LIMITING ROBOTS DEVELOPMENT FACTORS

JOHN LOK

Made with ♥ on the Notion Press Platform
www.notionpress.com

Contents

Foreword

Prepare

What factors can influence robots future continue development ? This book divides two part, first part discuss how AI can change market development to be better as well as second part discuss how Ai improves economic recession. Can apply robotics to bring advantages to change organizational structure in order to improve market development to be better in the future ? Different kinds of business organizations will encounter different kinds of challenges, e.g. cost increasing, staff shortage, reducing customers number or sale etc. challanges. So, when the organization can judge whether which aspects of weaknesses it is experiencing as well as it can know why and how to attempt to implement the most suitable or the best strategy to solve its challenge when it is facing. Then, the organization will have possible to continue to existen. Otherwise, if the organization can not find whether which aspects are its difficuties , it is facing. Then, it can not implement the most suitable strategy to solve its challenges. Then, it will be closed down in possible. In my this book, I shall attempt to indicate some organizational cases and find whether what weakness or difficulties it is facing. Then, I shall recommend the best strategy to attempt to help it to solve the kind of challenge, it is encountering. Any have interesting to learn business strategy students, they can learn new strategic knowledge to help these organizations to solve their challenges.

Nowadays, robotic had been applies to different aspect to bring benefits to satisfy humans needs, they may include any hospitals' surgeon rooms medical surgeon equipment aspect, hotel room food delivery or hotel front line customer service aspect, shopping center, leisure places cleaning task aspect, student educational service aspect, warehouse logistic goods transport delivery tasks aspect , even general restaurants kitchen cooking tasks aspect, lawyer and accountant firms general bookkeeping, law writing draft clerical tasks aspects etc. Can robotic invention help employers to improve efficiencies or raise productivities in order to raise economic growth or it can be replaced low-skillful workers to cause any low-skillful jobs are done by artificial robots to achieve many low skillful workers will lose jobs and unemployment ratio will be influenced to raise in our societies?

I write this first part aims to discuss whether future robotic invention may help our societies improve economic growth or it can bring recession. This book includes two parts to discuss, this part indicates what reasons to explain why robotics may influence our societies economic growth as well as second part indicates what reasons to explain why robotics may bring our social recession both in possible. Readers can make individual analysis to judge whether robotics can influence our social economic growth or it may bring recession more.

This book second part aims to explain why and how future artificial intelligent technology (big data gathering method) can be applied to assit businesses to predict why and when and how consumer behavior changes in service industry. I shall explain why traditional psychological and statistic and marketing methods are applied to predict consumer behaviors, human's judgement and analytical effort will be worse to compare AI machine's judgement and analytical effort in srvice industry. Also, I shall indicate different business organizations why they apply AI big data gathering method to help them to design any questionnaires (surveys) questions which will be more valid and useful to conclude human's questionnaires (surveys) design questions method to predict what service requirements can be satisfied to their potential service consumers' needs.Can apply (AI) learning machine predict what and how consumers service to satisfy their needs ? Can (AI) learning machine replace human marketing research method, e.g. survey or human psychological and micro and macro economic methods to predict consumers service needs more accurate?

In my this part, I concentrate on indicate whether any artificial intelligence (AI) tools will be one kind of good consumer behavioral prediction method to be choose to apply to predict consumer service needs. I shall indicate some examples, cases to give reasonable evidences to analyze whether (AI) tools will be one kind suitable tool to be applied to predict when and how consumer service needs changes. If (AI) can be one kind tool to attempt to be applied to predict when and how consumer service needs changes. Will it replace other kinds of methods to predict consumer service needs ? Does it have weaknesses to be applied to predict consumer behaviors, instead of strengths? Can it be applied to predict consumer behaviors depending on any situations of only some situation? Finally, I believe that any readers can find answers to answer above these questions in this book. In my analysis, I conclude marketing development or marketing change trend will be influenced by consumer behavioral change model or attitude factor. Finally, I hope my readers can give opinions to make judgement to evaluate my opinions whether is right or wrong in this research topic.

Prologue

Table of contents

CHAPTER ONE

Limiting (AI) prediction consumer behavior tool deve lopment

How can artificial intelligent tools predict consumer behavior in vehicle market

What is (AI) consumer behavioral prediction tool? How any why will (AI) tool assist manufactures to attempt to predict consumer behavior before and after consumption occurrence? First, I shall indicate how to apply (AI) tool to predict vehicle product consumer behavior case example.

Nowadays, many vehicle manufacturers hope their vehicles can attract to vehicle buyers to choose to buy their vehicles. However, there are many different brands of vehicles to provide to them to choose, so the vehicle market competition is very serious.

How to judge their different kinds of vehicle price which is reasonable acceptance to attract vehicle buyers to choose to buy the brand of vehicle manufacturers' any kinds of vehicles, e.g. fast speed sport style vehicles, comfortable and slow speed common cars, for four passengers common small size or more than four passengers common large car size? How to evaluate the vehicle prices issue is important factor to influence vehicle buyers' choices. Either if the brand of vehicle price is too high to compare brands, it will influence many vehicle buyers choose to buy other brands' vehicles or if the brand of vehicle price is too low, it will influence vehicle buyers feel this brand's vehicle's quality is worse to compare to other vehicle brands' similar vehicle products.

Thus, if the brand of vehicle manufacturers can predict how to design vehicles which can attract many vehicle buyers to choose to buy whose any vehicle products. What are future vehicle buyers' favorable vehicle styles? Then, the vehicle manufacturer can concentrate on manufacturing the kind style of vehicle products to sell already. It will reduce its vehicle manufacturing investment risk.

How to apply (AI) tools to predict vehicle buyers' behavioral consumption model? Whether artificial intelligent tools can predict automotive buyers' behavioral consumption model and predict future trend. In fact, automotive brands and dealerships are facing an increasingly competition when attempting to manually gathering the vast quantities of data required to create customer focused programs that increase retention, ultimately new sales and service automotive business. Building a based on that client's intrinsic needs and interests to any kinds of automotive vehicles at any given time. This is especially true in the automotive industry where the time span between purchases is measured in years. Because vehicle buyers would not like often to change their old vehicle to another new one. So, their decisions to buying another new vehicle, the time is usually after one year, even longer time. Hence, it seems any vehicles won't be frequent consumption products to the owned at least one vehicle family consumers (vehicle buyers).

Hence, how to predict vehicle consumers' taste or preferable which styles of vehicle choices issues is very important. If the vehicle manufacturers can not manufacture any attractive vehicles to sell easily in this year. Then, it will lose time, money in this year because it won't know when the owned least one vehicle users or non-owned any vehicle users who will decide to buy one new vehicle or change another new vehicle ensure. The different brand vehicle dealers will possible wait more than one year to attract them to buy their vehicles if their styles are not attractive to compare other brands of vehicle competitors.

However, artificial intelligence and machine learning can help any vehicle manufacturers to find solution to solve patterns in highly to solve patterns in highly complex data-sets that are beyond the capability of a human brain, and then building and automatically acting on the customer insights it generates.

Given the automotive customer need for individualized communications, this technology is positioned to become a critical component of any successful vehicle retailer's domestic or/and overseas vehicle markets. How can vehicle manufacturers and retailers use (AI) to enhance their vehicle

marketing campaigns? How will (AI) affect their vehicle sale marketing strategy? What criteria would they use when selecting on (AI) solution?
Vehicle consumers today are able to quickly access different brands of vehicle information, research vehicle products and reviews, negotiate prices and compare one vehicle brand or retailer to another resulting of the brands of vehicle customers. At the same time, the rise of " big -data mining", wearable devices that track user's every move and preference and greater contextualization in advertising and social media has resulted in consumer expectations of individualized. Thus, it seems that (AI) tools can be used to gather " big-data" and then they can make human's mind to analyze how to design kinds of vehicles to satisfy vehicle buyers' needs.
As automotive vehicle marketers can apply (AI) tools to achieve messaging strategies to meet the needs of this new generation of informed vehicle consumers, using data from a variety of sources to move from a variety of sources to move from mass- messaging to more personalized messages aimed at particular vehicle buyer segments, e.g. fast speed sport vehicle buyer segment, slow speed comfortable small size or large size of buyer segment. However, when 90% of vehicle marketers believe having a single vehicle buyer view is important, only 6% have achieved it.
However, one of the main issues vehicle marketers facing is the lack of capacity to efficiently sift through and analyze the massive vehicle buyer amounts of data required to create vehicle buyer individualized vehicle customer experiences easily. This is especially difficult for automotive dealers, the long periods between purchase cycles, and the highly considered nature of the vehicle purchase means that each vehicle dealer needs to not only track a large number of potential vehicle customers for an extremely long period of time, but each of those vehicle customers will generate a huge amount of different kinds of vehicle behavioral consumption data as they research their next vehicle purchase. However, by choosing the right (AI) technological tools and programs , vehicle dealers can solve this big data gathering challenge into a major advantage.
For Forrester vehicle brand example, vehicle consumers have more power over the Forrester vehicle brand's reputation than ever before. Mayne, L. (2014) indicated that Forrester calls this new (AI) tools is the " age of the vehicle customer", a 20 year business cycle in which the most successful vehicle enterprises will reinvent themselves to systematically understand and serve increasingly powerful vehicle consumers. To win in this new age, Forrester declares companies must become vehicle customer obsessed and

the only sustainable competitive advantage is knowledge and engagement with customers, such as (AI) gathering data knowledge.

Thus, the biggest challenge vehicle businesses currently face is not the collection of a large quantity of vehicle consumer data, but what to do with that data once they have it. Even at a large vehicle data research firm, the data sets are often too big for a single analyze, or even a team of analysts to sort through and draw conclusion from. However, enter artificial intelligence and machine learning , an efficient technology solution that can continuously find patterns in highly complex data sets that are way beyond the capacity of a human brain and then automatic drive action based on the customer insights is generated.

What is (AI) machine learning tool? Machine learning is a type of (AI) that learns from data and is not explicitly program. Think Amazon, face book. Machine learning serves up relevant content based on an individual vehicle purchase behavior and experiences. More simply, machine learning is a computer program that can learn relationships between data, subject those learnings to errors functions, and then learn from its errors. The program in effect, trains itself.

Lee, T. (2016) explained that "Thus, (AI) tools can learn deep a more advanced branch of machine learning inspired by how our brain's nervous function, has also been found to be especial effective in identifying patterns from data."

When this way sound is complicated from a vehicle dealer perspective, the implementation of a marketing program driven by artificial intelligence can take care of these tasks in an automatic vehicle fashion with little to no manual intervention required from the staff at time vehicle stores.

In practice at a vehicle dealership, the program will continue track vehicle customer behavior online, merging that data with any offline source (like CRM or DMS data) and then analyze this aggregated vehicle buyer data set to predict what vehicle customer may be shopping for and what information they might like to relevance from different kinds style of vehicle design photos.

1.1 Why can (AI) be applied to predict consumer behaviors?

Artificial intelligence refers to complex in vehicle market, machine learning that posses the same characteristics of human intelligence and that have all our sense, all our reason and think just like human do. Besides, machine learning is the practice of using algorithms to collect and examine data, learn from it, and then make a determination or prediction about something

in the world.
The machine is " trained" using large amounts of data and algorithms that give it the ability to learn how to automatically perform a task with increasing accuracy. Otherwise, deep learning is primarily based on artificial neural networks inspired by our understanding of the biology of human's brains.
Deep learning breaks down tasks in ways that enables machines to assist us with increasingly complex tasks, driverless cars, better preventive healthcare and more accurate product recommendation (including vehicle recommendations). So, such as why (AI) technology can be applied to predict how vehicle consumer behavior changes to bring to judge whether vehicle consumer will like what kinds of vehicle styles next year. Then, vehicle manufacturers can gather overall vehicle consumer data to analyze and conclude the more accurate vehicle design direction for next year any new design vehicle manufacturing products.
Thus, (AI) machine learning can help vehicle manufacturers to solve how to design any new vehicle products challenge. A vehicle is both one of the most important and carefully considered purchases the majority of people will ever make in their lifetime. It is also a purchase that tends to be fundamentally tied to a person's identify and view of themselves. As the same time, vehicle consumers changing lifestyles result in changing vehicle needs, e.g. the young sport car enthusiast matures into the family driver.
Automotive dealers need to remember that vehicle customers and prospects are individual human beings with risk, complex and ever-changing lives factors, these factors will influence every vehicle consumer why who feels has vehicle purchase need, and how who choose to buy the first vehicle if who decided to buy the first vehicle.
The (AI) technological customer behavioral prediction tool seems to be the best vehicle salespeople in the world are those that know every one of their vehicle customers. Their likes and dislikes which style of vehicle design, preferences and changing tastes to vehicle choices. The capacity of the human brain, however, limits us from achieving this type of vehicle sales and frequent turnover at vehicle dealerships often results in the further loss of vehicle salespeople along with their vehicle customer relationships and knowledge. In this competitive vehicle environment, machine learning enables platforms to assist the vehicle sales team by tracking the vehicle consumer behaviors of each vehicle customer, learning and memorizing their preferences and predicting their future vehicle purchase needs.

Finally, I recommend that for a vehicle dealerships marketing platform to make their customer engagement efficient and fully-functional, I should be able to: applying (AI) tools to track every vehicle customer behavior across the web, connecting to a society of data sources, CRM, DMS, third-party, web vehicle brands, social email, click etc., aggregating and accurately cross-reference data from a variety of sources, leveraging this data to drive insights on a mass scale, as well as on an individualized basis, driving actions and automatically direct customer engagement via multiple channels based on where each customer is in their individual lifecycle.

1.2 How can (AI) provide businesses with better-informed decisions

I shall explain how (AI) technology can provide businesses with better-informed decisions to drive top-line growth, deliver meaningful experience for customers and smooth their path along the consumer journey. The widely understood definition of (AI) involves the ability of machines or computers to learn human thinking, reasoning and decision-making abilities.

A Narrative science study in 2015 year identified that (AI) was being used primarily in voice recognition, machine learning virtual assistants and decision support. This study also highlighted the many branches of (AI) and that techniques and their definition are used interchangeably. It is possible that (AI) can be used to gather big data , then to analyze to help businesses to predict consumer behaviors. For example, one of the most common techniques is machine learning, where algorithms are used to perform tasks by learning from historical data. Another growth branch of (AI) is natural language procession.

However, during 2017 year, search engines will begin to factor additional behavioral data into prediction of customer behavioral results, such as the user's history of searches and locations and previously captures conservations. Artificial intelligence will use this information to power predictive search results, e.g. predictive future consumer's choice behavioral processing for any kinds of businesses.

Predictive search will improve the quality of search results, and provide new insights into consumers' behavior and the moments which matter to them. Search will give recommendation into tailored how consumer individual choice in consumption process. Several of the largest online platforms already use machine learning to improve predictive consumer behavioral search results.

For example, Google's rank brain technology adds research by understanding the context in which the consumer has entered it. Over time, rank brain will learn further from user behaviors Amazon's DSSTNE (pronouned destiny) learns from shoppers' purchasing habits and consumption behavior to offer better product recommend actions, which Amazon can offer before a consumer has entered anything into the search bar. However, this technology is not independent of human input. For example, Google engineers will periodically retain the rank brain system to improve the models it uses. For another example, in 2016 year , Apple computer revamped its photos app to allow consumers to search for specific items in the phots, they want to find, not just dates and locations. Each photo that an intelligent phone or intelligent pad user takes goes through 11 billion computations, so that photos can understand exactly what is the photography.

It seems that in future, (AI) machine learning will allow search to evolve even further. Search engineers will deliver refined recommendations to their business users and use less human input to predict consumers' needs. For IBM computer example, it indicated 90% of the data that exists today has been created in the last two years. This huge explosion of data gives brands the opportunity to quickly spot and react to the latest trends, fashion and fads among its clients and potential clients. This will allow companies to better engage with younger consumers, who gain influence access to the latest trends, and use the brands. They associate with to help define who they are as individuals. Thus, brands have to identify and make use of them before consumers move on, but the vast quantity of data available makes. This a resource-intensive task. For next example, Lesara, a based online clothes store, uses this machine learning to inform its product decision often gathering information from internal and external sources. When its trends -spotting shoes. Lesara has a range of over 20 styles and sells hundreds of pairs a day. It focus on giving consumers, the very latest trends allow Lesara to develop on average of 50,000 new items each year. It compared to 11,000 old items each year. Thus, (AI) brain seems to human brain to own analytical ability to predict consumer behaviors.

For another example, Lesara is one online clothes store, uses machine learning decisions after gathering information from internal and external sources. One of its most popular products, shoes with LED started life when its trend spotting software flagged up a blogger wearing similar shoes. Now Lesara has a range of over 20 styles and sells hundreds of pairs a day. Its focus on giving consumers the very latest trends allows Lesara to develop an average of 50,000 new items each year, compared to 11,000 for its competitor Lara. it seems (AI) machine learning can help Lesara business to predict what kinds of shoes design or style that shoe consumers will prefer choose to buy in future shoe market trend. Thus, Lesara can predict shoe consumers' taste successfully and it can manufacture many attractive style of shoes. (AI) machine learning can gather global past shoe consumer's shoe shopping experiences, then analyzes to make conclusion to give lesara recommendation successfully. This will make the experience more enjoyable for shoe consumers and allow Lesara to advert whose different new style or design of shoes to deliver them move relevant messages by understanding the context of the experience.

However, (AI) machine learning will have this risk who manufacturers need to concern if they applied this technology to predict consumer behavior. It is on sample consumers' privacy issue, in order to avoid complaint chance occurrence. However, machine learning can tie this data together to identify which f the billions of devices are being used by individual consumers. This helps brands understand how consumer engagement and actions can be attributed to different messages in different contexts and at different time. So, machine learning can help brands to build confidence to promote their products by any advertisement channels. When, this new (AI) machine learning technology can conclude how to design their products to be the most attractive, due to it has more accurate to predict consumer behaviors to compare human themselves prediction judgement effort. It seems that (AI) machine judgement effort is more accurate to compare to human judgment effort.

For example, google is moving away from cookies and using logged in data to track and make to users. It plans to expand the scope of the brand lift tool from online video. Thus, consumers are responded will to shippable context, finding it persuasive and easy to navigate by (AI) machine learning decision. For example, fashion brands can aggregate their You tub videos and blogs into a mobile context marketing experience, such as brand centric context into a personal shopping activity gives the shopper an experience, who are likely to remember and tell their friends about any new style of products design promotion from these internet advertisement channels after (AI) machine learning tools' styles of product design recommendation.

What is (AI) deep learning techniques to forecast environment behavioral consumption

The (AI) deep-learning technology leads to performance enhancement and generalization of artificial intelligent technology. It influences the global leader in the field of information technology has declared its intention to utilize the deep-learning technology to solve environmental problems, such as climate change. So, it will help agriculture farming businesses can raise any plant food: vegetable, fruit, rice which grow up very easily if farmers can apply (AI) deep-learning technology to solve environment problems to influence their plant food grow. If the whole year seasonal change is very good and it is suitable for any plant food to grow in farming land easily, e.g. rain is enough and soil is enough for any plant food to grow in the farm lands. Then, fruit, rice, vegetable etc. agriculture businesses will have much beneficial attribution to global farmers.

The question is how to use deep-learning technologies in the environmental field to predict the status of pro-environmental consumption. We predicted the pro-environmental consumption index based on Google search query data, using a recurrent neural network (RNN model). To certify the accuracy of the index, we compared the prediction accuracy of thc RNN model with that of the ordinary least square and artificial necessary network models. For example, the RNN model predicts the pro-environmental consumption index better than any other model. we expect the RNN model to perform still better in a big data environment because the deep-learning technologies would be increasingly as the volume of data grows. So, deep-learning technologies could be useful in environmental forecasting to prevent damage caused by climate change to influence any rice, vegetable, tomato, potato, fruit etc. different plant food grow in any countries' farming land easily.

For South Korea example, over 800 government agencies spent 2.2 trillion Korea won on eco-products in 2014 year. However, green products are rarely purchased outside these agencies. This phenomenon occurs because there is a gap between consumer attitudes and behavior , that is environmental attitudc is a major factor in dccision making vis a vis the consumption of " green" food and services (Jorea Ministry of Environment, 2015). Therefore, it is necessary to understand those consumer attitude, that will lead to sustainability-conductive behavior and consumption.

2.1 Environmental consumption prediction

Recently, many researchers have studied pro-environmental consumption and household indexes as well as suicide rate predictions using messages posted by internet users on Google trend, Tweets etc. channel. Whether can environmental consumption be predicted by (AI) deep-learning technological internet channel? How can impact the pro-environmental consumption attitudes of green policies? Korea scientists estimated pro-environmental attitudes using search query data provided by Google trend and confirmed through regression analysis, that pro-environmental attitude has a positive correlation with the pro-environmental attitude index. They also explained that environment-friendly attitude of residents plan an important role in policy making. In the past, most household consumption indexed were calculated through surveys, but (AI) deep-learning technological tool " big data" have recently gained research attention (Lee et al. 2016).

It seems that (AI) deep-learning technology can help agricultural export countries‘ farmers , e.g. US, UK, Canada, New Zealand, Australia, Japan, China, India etc. they can predict environmental behavioral consumption to any rice, tomato, potato , fruit, vegetable etc. plant food consumers. The beneficial advantages to them include as below:

(a) Assuming they know their countries' weather, when it has less rain to cause drought or when it has more rain in any seasonal time in the year. They can choose not to grow any kinds of above these plant food to avoid loss.

(b) They can make any kinds of above these plant food price raising after their prediction of these bad seasonal time to cause their plant food shortage supply challenge. Because these plant food consumers‘ demand number is more, but the supply of these above plant food supply number is less. However, due to they had predicted when the bad seasonal time can not allow them to grow these above plant food before. So, they have enough time to grow many these above plant food number in predictive good seasonal time to prepare to supply to their plant food import countries' plant food consumers to eat. Thus, these predictive environmental consumption plant food export countries can raise their plant food price to sell to them. When, the other non-pre-predictive environmental consumption plant food export countries can not supply any one of those plant food to them to eat, due to the bad climate to cause them can't grow any one of these plant food to export to sell.

Thus, (AI) deep-learning technology can be applied to predict how to raise the plant food supply number in order to raise price to the import plant food countries consumers to eat, due to they feel difficult to buy these plant food to eat in the bad climate seasonal time in whole year.

(c) (AI) deep-learning technology can help climate scientists to find what reasons cause their countries; rain sudden increases or cause their countries‘ rain sudden decreases. After its gathering data analysis, it can assist climate scientists to find solution methods to attempt to control the rain level can be right falling down level to let agricultural export farmers who can grow their plant food to sell to agricultural import countries in whole year.

(d) The agricultural export countries’ farmers can apply (AI) deep-learning technology to help them to choose whether growing which kinds of plant food in that whether climate time to earn more plant food consumption number more easily.

Due to the agricultural countries climate will often change, for example, tomato, potato, rice, fruit etc. plant food can be adapt to grow in more rain time, but vegetable can not be adapt to grow in more rain time. If farmers can apply this technology to predict when it will have move rain or when it will have less rain to fall down in their countries. Then, they can choose to grow which kinds of plant food number more, in the suitable seasonal climate time in order to raise plant food growing number productivities to supply to sell to satisfy any agricultural food import countries‘ demand effectively.

(e) (AI) deep-learning technology can help agricultural import countries to solve agricultural food shortage challenge in long term. When this technology can be popular to base applied by the agricultural plant food export countries. It will solve global agricultural food shortage challenge. For example, when one agricultural export countries’ farmers can popular accept to apply this technology to predict when to grow which kinds of plant food more to rise number productivities to sell. e.g. vegetable, fruit, rice Besides another agricultural export countries‘ farmers can also accept to apply this technology to predict when to grow plant food, e.g. potato, tomato to raise number productivities to sell. Then, they can concentrate on growing the specific kinds of plant food in order to raise the specific plant food number productivities in every seasonal change time every month. Then, global agricultural plant food supply must be raised, due to these predictive environmental change farmers can know who ought grow which kinds of plant food to sell to raise number productivities.

2.2 How can apply (AI) digital channel to predict consumer behaviors?

(AI) digital channel can be applied to help businesses to evaluate whether how much the product price is the most attractive to persuade consumers feel it is the most reasonable price to sell. It helps consumers to feel which brands of products which ought change the price to let consumers to choose to buy the brand of product. It can be applied to predict whether how many consumer numbers can be increased or decreased when the brand of product's price is variable. It aims to give opinions to help any brand of product manufacturers or sellers to judge whether which price is the most reasonable to let consumers to accept to choose to buy the brand of product in popular.

Thus, (AI) price measurement technology can be preference to be applied online communication ecommerce and mobile phone internet platform aspect. As businesses can enter their past products prices data and past customer number data into computer or mobile. Then, (AI) price measurement technology can gather these data to analyze these product prices and past customer number to compare their prices variable changing range level to find their price variable difference to measure to make conclusion about every product's price variable changing will influence how many customer number increase or decrease changing to choose to sell their different kinds of products more accurate. Then, (AI) price measurement software will help them to analyze all past price variable changing data to compare whether which price range can let customers to feel it is more reasonable and attractive to influence them to choose to buy the product among different brands of product choice.

Because any product's price is one important factor to influence consumers to choose to buy the product, instead of quality, durability, shape, appearance, color, brand familiarity etc. factors. Any online businesses with a focus on Asia should considerate (AI) customer care, and virtual shopping experience, whereas is Europe and North America still value face-to-face and/or real human interaction over (AI) or virtual worlds.

For example, Amazon publish has applied (AI) price measurement technology to help authors to decide how much every different topic of e-book or paper book price, it can attract the largest number of readers to buy. Any one author only needs to type whose book name to Amazon publish author himself/herself Amazon website. Amazon publish (AI) price measurement learning machine will help them to auto-calculate and judge how much e-book or paper book price is the most attractive and the most reasonable in order to increase reader number to buy their e-books or paper books to read. So, (AI) online price measurement machine will gather past similar book names and past every similar book readers' reading times and the number of readers to give opinions to let every author to judge whether his/her very new e-book or paper book ought charge how much price to the e-book or paper book which can attract many readers to choose to buy. Although, it is not ensure that the e-book or paper book price must let readers to feel it is the most reasonable price to choose to buy in reader's view point. However, it has other factors to influence readers‘ choice to buy the e-book or paper book, e.g. whether the book content is attractive to public, the author's familiarity, the book's page is enough or not to satisfy readers to read etc. factors. But, instead of all these extra factors to influence readers to choose to buy the book to read. (AI) price measurement learning machine can real give opinions to every author to let them to judge the e-book or paper book different price range whether is too high to influence readers to choose to buy to read or tool low to influence readers feel it is possible poor content book to compare other similar content books. Thus, (AI) price measurement machine can help authors to predict every reader's reading behaviors or reading experience and reading habit from online channel in short time easily. The author only enter the book name to let Amazon publish price measurement machine to check, it will follow past reader's reading habit and reading experience to judge whether the similar all book topic sale record to judge how much price is the reasonable price to attract many readers to buy the book.

Hence, (AI) can be applied to digital channel to help businesses to predict consumer behavior in the future. In the future, mobile/smartphone, laptop, desktop will be most frequent used ecommerce channels to develop online business. So, (AI) can be also applied to these platforms to gather data to make analysis to help businesses to predict consumer purchase behaviors popularly. Due to , ecommerce is popular to global, so digital online and instore channels can be one good channel to let (AI) learning machine to make platform to gather past every online consumer purchase (buying) experience data to help businesses to build brand personality and having a responsible, positive impact on society.

To apply (AI) learning machine technology to understand customer online purchase behavior, it will raise business e-commerce successful chance: For example, (AI) learning machine can help businesses to gather data to analyze to determine whether short-term or long-term signals in the online consumer behavior that indicate higher purchase intents to let every online business to know. (AI) learning machine can find that online users with long-term purchasing intent tend to save and click through on more content. However, as online users approach the time of purchase their activity becomes more topically focused and actions shift from saves to searches from online consumption channel. Then, (AI) learning machine will further find that the brand product purchase signals in online behavior can exist weakness before an online purchase is made and can also be traced across different online purchase categories. Finally, (AI) learning machine synthesize these insights in predictive models of online user purchasing intent to the brand of product. Taken together, it's work identifies a set of general principles and signals that can be used to model online user purchasing intent across many online content discovery applications. Thus, (AI) learning machine can help online businesses to gather any online users' click online behaviors data to judge whether there are how many online users will choose to find their online business websites to make final decisions to buy their products from online channels. Then, it will give opinions to help the online businesses to let it to judge whether what are the important website factors will help its online business to attract many online consumers, e.g. designing unattractive website issue, online unattractive product photos issue, unclear website color issue, unclear website advertisement message, contents and words impressions issue, lacking image movement frequent attractive seeing issue etc. different website factors. Thus, online digital channel will be one good choice to apply (AI) learning machine to help businesses to predict consumer behaviors.

2.3 Can apply artificial intelligent learning machine " big data" gathering method to predict manufacturers‘ behavioral performance ?

In consumer view point, can they apply (AI) learning machine to predict manufacturers' behavioral performance to judge whether whose products are value to buy. Nowadays, (AI) and big data are reshaping the risk in consumer privacy. For example, consumers want to hide their willingness to pay just as firms want to hide their real marginal cost, and buyers have less favorable information, say a low credit shore, prefer to withhold it just as sellers want to conceal poor product quality. So, it implies that it is possible (AI) learning machine can help customers to gather any manufacturers‘

past sale performance, e.g. how many complaints or appreciation from clients, product quality etc. sale data to let consumers to make judgement whether it is value to buy to compare other competitors. So, it has risk to the poor product quality of manufacturers. Otherwise, it has benefits to the good product quality of manufacturers. It also implies all manufacturers' privacy is not protected or secret when (AI) learning machine is popular to be used to predict manufacturers' behaviors by consumers.

Information economists suggest that both buyers and sells have an incentive to hide or reveal private information, and these incentives are crucial for market efficiency. Data technology that reveals consumers type could facilitate a better match between product and consumer type, and data technology that helps buyers to assess product quality could encourage high quality production.

Thus, (AI) big data technology can also assist consumers to gather different manufacturers' data to compare what their advantages and disadvantages of their products are. Then, consumers can make comparison to choose which brand of product is the suitable to whom to buy in these more choice consumption market. (AI) learning machine will gather similar brand their products' data to analyze to make conclusion to let consumers know or feel to make final judge to find what advantages or disadvantages of these sample brands of similar products' comparison from internet. On the other hand, it means that manufacturers can gather consumers' past purchase behaviors or purchase experience from (AI) big data gathering method to record and analyze to give opinions to let manufacturers to know what reasons or factors influence consumers choose not to buy their products from internet.

(AI) big data gathering consumer behavior prediction method can give these benefits to manufacturers and consumers both, such as: New concerns arise because (AI) technological advance which have enables reducing cost of collecting, storing, processing and using data in mass quantities extend information beyond a single transaction. These advances are often summarized by the big data, it means charge volume of transaction-level data that could identify individual consumers by itself or in combination with the datasets.

The popular (AI) takes big data as in input in order to understand, predict and influence consumer behavior. Modern (AI) is used by legitimate companies, could improve management efficiency motivate innovations and better match demand and supply. But (AI) in the wrong hand, also allows the mass production of fraud and deception. Since , data can be stored, traded and used long after the transaction. Future data use is likely to grow with data processing technology, such as (AI) big data gathering consumer and manufacturer behavioral prediction method from internet channel.

Thus, future (AI) big data learning machine can also help consumers to choose the best brand of manufacturer's products among different brands of manufacturers products choice to compare their past sale performance from internet. They can apply (AI) big data statistic method to gather all different manufacturers' similar products past sale data to compare their advantages and disadvantages to make the best decision to choose to buy which brand of product is the most suitable to them to buy to use. It seems (AI) big data can also help consumers to predict any manufacturers' manufacturing behaviors or manufacturing performance whether they are improving their product quality or are deteriorating their product quality. Thus, (AI) big data tool is also important to help customers to predict future the different brands of manufacturer performance will have improvement in possible.

Thus, I believe that artificial intelligent "big data" gathering method can be suggested to be applied to attempt to predict consumer behavioral changes in global business environment, the reasons are as below:

On the consumer's beneficial hand, Consumers can apply this method to attempt to gather any global manufacturers data to be analyzed by this artificial intelligent learning system. Then, it analyzed all the different brands of specific similar product manufacturer' data to compare what are the range of the best past manufacturing history and sale data to the group of best manufacturers, and what are the range of the better past manufacturing history and sale data, and what are the range of the good past manufacturing history and sale data, and what are the range of the common past manufacturing history and sale data. Finally, the (AI) learning system will compare all the specific similar product, e.g. mobile phone or computer, television, car etc. different kinds of specific products of global manufacturers to conclude the result is such as whether which brands will be the best manufacturers to let the consumer to buy the television or mobile phone or computer or car etc. different kinds of products. It can make more accurate judgement to compare general human's phone or questionnaire surveys investigation method, newspapers, television, radios, Internet searches etc. different manufacturing news or data gathering channels to find which brands are the most worth confidence to consumers to choose to buy the specific product in the global consumption market.

On the manufacturers' beneficial hand, manufacturers can apply (AI) data gathering method to predict consumer emotion and buying behavioral changes more accurate. For example, the vehicle manufacturer, it plans to gather data to predict potential driving fast speed sport vehicle consumers' preferences trends in order to make the accurate judgement how to design its sport vehicles to attract many sport vehicle buyers who will choose to buy it's brand of any driving fast speed sport vehicles. It can attempt to apply (AI) intelligent learning system to gather global different brands of sport vehicle data concerns that all past driving fast speed sport vehicle buyer's preference of sport vehicle design. Then, the (AI) intelligent learning system gather global different brands of driving fast speed sport vehicle which had ever been purchased by the different country's driving fast speed sport vehicles consumers. After, it can compare divide the range of similar driving fast speed sport vehicle design and similar price to be different groups. The (AI) intelligent learning system can attempt to follow the past number of different brands of driving fast speed sport vehicle buyers to calculate how many driving fast speed sport vehicle buyers who choose to buy the brand of driving fast speed sport vehicle as well as it will analyze and make judgement to find whether the cheaper price reason attracts the different countries sport vehicle buyers choose to buy the brand of driving fast speed sport vehicle or the attractive design reason attracts the different countries sport vehicle buyers choose to buy the brand of sport vehicle or fast speed reason attracts the sport vehicle buyers choose to buy the brand of sport vehicle.

For example, although some brands of driving fast speed sport vehicle manufacturers' prices are very high, but they can still attract global many sport vehicle consumers to buy. Whether all sport vehicle's attractive design is the main factor to influence them to buy or whether it's fast speed is the main factor to influence them to buy or whether it's safe confidence it the main factor to influence them to buy or it's familiarity brand is the main factor to influence them to buy. (AI) intelligent learning system will attempt to make judgement and analysis to conclude whether the attractive design factor is the main factor to influence many sport vehicle consumers to choose to buy the brand of sport vehicles.

Otherwise, for another example, although some brands of driving fast speed sport vehicle manufacturer's prices are low, but they can not still attract many global many sport vehicle consumers to buy. Whether all vehicle's unattractive design is the main factor to influence them choose not to buy their fast speed driving sport vehicles or whether the unsafe factor is the main factor to influence them choose not to buy their fast speed driving sport vehicles or whether unfamiliarity brand is the main factor to influence many consumers choose not to buy their fast speeding sport vehicles.

Thus, when (AI) learning system had helped the fast speed sport vehicles manufacturer to gather all different brands of fast speed driving sport vehicle's past sale data and price data, design of different sport vehicle, e.g. color choice, method of style, comfortable chair styles and chair sizes and what kinds of steel material to manufacture the sport vehicles data and driving safe and accident occurrence data and the data concerns what reasons of the past complaint to brand of sport vehicle manufacturer from its sport vehicle buyers. Then, it can make more conclusion to give more accurate opinions whether which brands of fast speed driving sport vehicle manufacturer(s) whose sport vehicle design is the main factor to attract consumers choose to buy its any driving fast speed sport vehicle products really. Thus, it seems that it can make more accurate judgement to compare television survey, questionnaire survey to gather data concerns how to design the fast speed sport vehicle to attract consumers to choose to buy the sport vehicle manufacturer's planning sport vehicle products. I believe that (AI) learning system can help the sport vehicle manufacturer to make more accurate conclusion or judgement how to design its fast speed driving sport vehicles to attract it's consumers more easily.

CHAPTER TWO

Main barriers influence artificial intelligence consumer behavioral prediction

In future, it is possible that these barriers will influence how to apply (AI technology) to predict consumer behavior in success. The barriers may include: Lacking of a (AI) digital data gathering vision and strategy, lacking of efficient workforce readiness, (AI) technology constraints., non reaching (AI) consumer behavioral prediction mature stage, time and money and resource constraints, law and regulations prohibition to develop (AI) consumer behavioral prediction bug data gather technology.

However, the recommendation of solutions to attack the barriers to influence artificial intelligence consumer behavioral prediction not success, it may include gaining employee buy in to participate and develop (AI) consumer behavioral prediction technology, making customer experience to a concern (AI) big data gather questionnaire investigation, providing compensation, training to employees in order to achieve (AI) consumer behavioral big data questionnaire investigation research digital technological goals and strategy, task senior leaders manage any (AI) digital big data gather technology changes, putting policies and (AI) big data gather digital technology in place to support a fully remote, flexible workforce in any (AI) digital big data gather questionnaires research projects, teaching all employees how to code/understand (AI) big data gather consumer behavioral prediction software development, appointing a chief (AI) officer to manage any (AI) big data gather customer behavioral prediction projects and automate everything and encourage customers to attempt experience to self-service and (AI) big data gather questionnaire research to earn beneficial consumption aim after they gave feedback to any (AI) digital questionnaire researches. So, in the future, the (AI) digital big data questionnaire researches can include these industries surveyed, such as automat m financial services, public healthcare, private healthcare, technology, telecoms, insurance, life sciences, manufacturing, media and entertainment , oil and gas, retail and consumer products etc.

Hence, in the future, any of these industries can attempt to apply (AI) digital big data gather technology to predict how and why consumer behaviors will change in order to avoid reducing consumer number threat occurrence.

6.1 (AI) digital data gather technology predicts food consumer behavior's main barriers

What are the main barriers to food industry? When the food manufacturer applies (AI) big data gather technology to predict food consumer behavior? The barriers include that the food manufacturer / provider needs to decide whether when the right time is applied to the right (AI) digital big data prediction tool channel to find the right food consumers to be chose to full food consumption satisfactory questionnaires, how to gather multi-class food consumption classifiers on real-world food consumers transactional data from the food sale domain consistently to show the critical numbers of different kinds of food items at which the predictive performance most accurate? So, any food manufacturer / provider's advanced in (AI) digital data gather warehousing and management technologies can provide that opportunities for food business to enhance long term relationship with the food providers' clients.

However, food industry's (AI) digital data gather aims to improve food customer product targeting, increase food customer loyalty and food purchase probability to the food supplier. To effective identify, understand and satisfy the needs of their food customers, the food suppliers need to develop the right (AI) digital questionnaire questions and find the right food customers to fill every right questions from every digital questionnaire at the right time through the right channel.

Above of all these, they will be the barriers when one food supplier expects its (AI) digital data gather questionnaires which can conclude the most accurate prediction concerns any kinds of consumer food product choices. So, such as (AI) digital data prediction model, it is needed to incorporate into the food market segmentation, food customer targeting, and food challenging decisions with the goal of maximizing the total food customer lifetime. For example, (AI) big data gather transaction data is reasonable and accurate for building predictive models. Transaction data can be electronically collected and readily made available for data mining in lot quantity at minimum extra costs.

Suggestion to apply (AI) prototypes of food customer profiles method to predict food customer behavioral changes. Prototypes of food customer profiles mean to be extracted from the discovered bins and multi-class classifies models are built using those prototypes. The learned models can than be used to predict the class of food customer profiles (e.g. restaurants, school canteens, supermarkets etc. food suppliers) based on their food purchases. The approach is validated on the case study of a food retail and food service company operating in food and beverages market.

So, a food customer profile, it is a description (AI) data gather tool will record every of food customer using available information, which help in understanding their background and food consumption behavior. (AI) data gather tool can well develop every food customer profile, every food customer data is essential in food market analysis as they aid food suppliers in saving time and money by highlighting the real potential food consumers whose needs are to be met rather a range of individuals.

So, (AI) data gather tool can record every food consumer profile and every can be factual or behavioral food consumption. A factual food customer profile consists of a set of characteristics for (AI) big data gather record, e.g. demographic information , such as food customer name, gender, birth date, when a behavioral food customer profile consists of what the food customer is actually doing and is usually derived from (AI) digital transactional data gather record.

So, (AI) big data gather record's every behavioral food consumer profile can be much stronger predictor of the future food supplier consumption choice actions of a food customer. Furthermore, the food supplier's (AI) all past food consumer information that make up demographically based all past food customer profiles are expensive to acquire when the information for the food suppliers' past every food consumer food consumption behaviors. Moreover, food customer profile can be recorded to make real food purchase every time. So, when the food supplier finds the past food consumer's record from (AI) big data gather tool. Then, it can make more accurate judgement whether past every food consumer has chose to buy its food to eat how many times every year in order to predict whether its every past food consumer will choose to buy its foods how many times next year in possible. If the next year, its every past food consumer's consumption time to the food supplier is less than its current year consumption time. Then, the food supplier can attempt to find whether what factors to cause the past food consumers do not choose to increase food purchase times to the food supplier in current year. The factors may be possible be the food supplier's food prices are raised, food quality or taste is poor, the different kinds of food supply is shortage challenge, the food supplier's consumers lose confidence to buy the food supplier's foods to eat, when (AI) big data gather tool can help the food suppliers to find what the main factors to cause the past food consumer number to be reduced in order to predict how future food consumers' behavioral changes will be influenced from the food supplier's competitors in the global food supply market. Hence, (AI) big data gather tool can help every food supplier to attempt to find what the main factors to case the food supplier's food consumer number to be reduced as well as it can help the food supplier to predict how the food supplier's potential (past not every purchase its any food consumers) food consumers who can be persuaded to choose to buy its foods to eat by learning what the main factors influence.

In conclusion, (AI) big data gather tool can help the food supplier to find what the main factors influence its past food consumers do not choose to buy its food more times or find what the main factors will attract its potential (not ever buying its foods consumes) food consumers to choose to buy the food supplier's foods to eat.

6.2 The challenges of (AI) big data gather shaping the future of retail for consumer industries

Another challenge of (AI) big data gather is that how to shape the consumer behavior to let business owner to feel or know oe predict. It means that how it express it's conclusion or opinion for every consumer behavior after it had gather all big data in any data gather period, e.g. three months, half year or one year consumer shopping model data gather period.

Because every kind of industry, consumers will continue to demand price and quality change , with a wide range of convenient fulfilment options among of different kinds of products or services supply. Overall, the (AI) big data gather procedure gives opinion concerns every time retail experience will become more exciting, simple and convenient, depending on the consumer's ever-changing needs. So, I believe that (AI) big data gather every conclusion or result will be different, due to consumer's price and quality demand will often change to every kind of product or service supply in retail industry. So, how to shape (AI) big data gathering's analytical conclusion or result more clear. I shall recommend organizations need to build great understanding of and a stronger connection to increasingly empowered consumers before they plan and implement how to apply (AI) big data gather tool to predict consumer behavior as below:

Firstly, (AI) is empowered by technology, the consumer is redefining value. The traditional measures of cost, choice and convenience are still relevant, but not control and experience are also important. Globally, consumers have access to more than 2 billion different products choice by a wide range of traditional competitors and dynamic new entrants, all experimenting with new business models and methods of client engagement.

As choice increases, loyalty becomes more difficult familiarity and the consumer becomes more empowered. Businesses will have no choice and constantly innovate and disrupt themselves by meeting new technologies of high standards and expectations of consumers. So, (AI) data gather tool will need to follow different target group of consumers' needs to follow their different kinds of product design or style choice preferable to gather data in order to conclude the different target groups of consumer behavior to give opinion more clear and accurate to let businessmen to understand more clear how its customers' behavioral choice trend in the future half month, even to two years period.

Secondly, businessmen need to adopt changing technologies rapidly. Technology will be the key driver of this retail industry. Industry participants will only success if they have a clear prediction to focus on how to using technology to increase the value added to consumers. They must , however, do so will I realistic assessment of their costs and benefits. Hence, (AI) big data gather technological tools will need to design to help them to gather data efficiently by these ways, such as the internet of things (IOT), artificial intelligence (AI) machine learning, augmented reality (AR)/virtual reality (VR), digital traceability. So, future (AI) big data gather tool are predicted to be most influential customer behavioral positive emotion changing tool for retail , due to their widespread applications , ability to drive efficiencies and impact on labor in order to impact consumer behavior changing effort from negative emotion to positive.

Thirdly, (AI) big data gather tool is an advanced data science of consumer behavior predictive tool. Businesses will have to bring the journey from simply collecting consumer data to using it to scale and systematize enhanced decision making across the entire value chain. When focused on their business goals, industry players should not lose sight of the impact that future capabilities and transformative business models may have on society.

However, (AI) big data gather tool will encounter these challenges when any business plans and implements to apply it to predict consumer behavior in retail industry. The challenges include that as below:

1. The high cost and difficulty of implementing new technologies . The (AI) big data gather tool needs capital and capabilities to be designed to implement to be applied to different retail industry users. so, expensive barriers to innovation, an organization and the skillsets of its people to support a new design of (AI) big data gather tool, highly digital technology may be required.

2. Slow pace of cultural change. Consumers need to adapt or accept (AI) new technology consumption model in the traditional retail industry. The rate of change is outpacing the ability of businesses to keep up. (AI) big data gather tool needs to be designed to adopt in new or evolved business model requires, in most cases, a new level of customer behavioral predictive machine operation will impact to influence any retail businesses' consumer behavioral changes at a minimum, an organization's structure, capabilities, culture and decision making. If the retail business expects to apply (AI) big data gather tool to predict how to change its consumer behaviors and how their consumption behaviors will tend to change in order to achieve to change their positive emotion from negative emotion before they choose to buy its product or consume its service in success.

6.3 Challenge to using (AI) neural networks to predict customer behavior from big data gather tool

(AI) big data gather tool will encounter the challenge: How can predict customer behavior be represented as sequential data describing the interactions of the customer with a company or an (AI) data gather system through the time, e.g. these interactions are items that the customer purchase or views ? So, every customer data gather , (AI) needs to spend time to analyze how and why to cause whose consumption behavioral choice. It is too difficult matter or judgement for (AI) learning. So, (AI) needs to spend time to learn how to analyze every customer's shopping behavior or actin in order to gather all different consumers' past shopping action information in order to help business owners to predict future its potential customer shopping behavior how to change more clear and accurate prediction.

(AI) big data gather tool needs to learn to know that how to judge every customer interaction likes purchases over time can be represented with sequential data. Sequential data has the main property that the order of the information is important. Many (AI) machine learning models are not suited for sequential data, as they consider each input sample independent from previous ones. Therefore, at the end of the sequence, (AI) big data gather learn machines need to keep in their internal state of every customer purchase data, kind of product or service, price , whole year consumption times form all previous inputs, making them suitable for this type of data.

However, consumer behavior can be represented as sequential data describing the interactions through the time. Examples of these interactions are the items that the user purchases or views. Therefore, the history of interactions can be modeled as sequential data, which has the particular trial that an incorporate a temporal aspect. For example, if a user buys a new mobile phone, who might purchase accessories for this mobile phone in the near future or it the user buys a electronic book or paper book , he might be interested in books by the same author. Therefore, to make accurate predictions is important to model this temporal aspect correctly. To solve this predictive challenge of consumers to buy the product. One count the number of purchased products of a particular category in the last N days, or the number of days since the last purchase.

So, the (AI) big data gather designers can attempt to produce a feature vector which can be fed into a machine learning algorithm such as " logistic regression" will be the main feature and function to any (AI) big data gather machine to learn how to apply this " logistic regression" function or feature to predict any customer behavioral change for any product purchase or service consumption to the (AI) predictive consumer behavioral business users. Every different kinds of product purchases or services consumption will be needed to design " different model of logistic regression" in order to follow the kind of business to predict whose consumer purchase or service consumption behavior to predict more accurate.

6.4 Challenges of artificial intelligence, algorithms technology and machine learning impact to consumption market

Markets have played a key role in providing individuals and businesses with the opportunity to gain from trade. If (AI) big data gather tool can predict how to change potential customer behavior in success. The challenges to consumers will face that the overall market consumption model will be dominated by the businessmen only. So, it is not fair or reasonable to consumers, because (AI) big data gather tool has controlled or dominated all consumers' minds and it has predicted how and why every kind of product or service consumer shopping model or consumption behaviors how will change.

It will bring this questions: How can market designers learn the characteristics necessary to set optimal, or at least better, reserve prices after they had gather all data to conclude the analytical results of their consumers behaviors how will change? How can market designers better learn the environments of their markets?

In response to these challenges, artificial intelligence (AI) and machine learning are important tools for market design. For example, retailers and marketplaces , such as eBay, Amazon and many others are mining their vast amounts of data to identity patterns that help them create better shopping experiences for their clients and increase the efficiency of their markets. By having better prediction tools, these and their companies can predict and better manage dynamic consumption market environments. The improved forecasting that (AI) and machine learning algorithms provide help marketplaces and retailers better anticipate consumer demand and producer supply as well as help target products and activities for segmented markets. Another important application of (AI) 's strength in improving forecasting to help markets operate more efficiently is in electricity market example. To operate efficiently, electricity marker makers can attempt to apply (AI) machine learning tool to follow every household family electricity consumers' past electricity consumption record to judge (predict) how it will be every family's forecasting in the year.

An inaccurate forecast in the electricity supply and demand that can dramatically affect electricity market bad supply outcomes causing high variance in electricity charge prices or worse, blackouts. By better predicting every family's electricity demand and supply , electricity market makers can better allocate power generation to the most efficient power sources and maintain a more reasonable electricity stable charge market. Any example is design market, the application of (AI) algorithms to market design are already widespread and diverse.

(AI) algorithms technology , it is a safe that (AI) will play a growing role in the design and implementation of market over a wide range of applications. The challenges are that how (AI) can guarantee accurate to predict when and why and how consumer behavioral changes to any retail industries. In fact, retailers will need to discover the value that (AI) can bring to what benefits to influence their customer behaviors.

In the future, (AI) will bring their benefits to influence customers to build positive emotions to any retailers in these aspects as below:

1. Future (AI) big data gather tool will be an area of compute science that deals with giving machines , the ability to seem like they have human intelligence. In short, it is the power of a machine to copy intelligent human behavior. For examaple, machine learning algorithms are being integrated into analytics and customer relationship management platforms to uncover information on how to better serve customers, chat bots have been incorporated into websites to provide immediate service to customers.

2. (AI) adoption continue to rise with chat bots taking the lead. Due to increasing ease of deployment , instant availability and improved quality, chat bots will become more and more common to manage customer service queries and to make intelligent purchase recommendations. Also, retailers can engage this kind of technology to answer continue questions and supplement customer support with chat-based shopping experience. So, (AI) and declines personalized, customized and localized experiences to customers.

(AI) will be applied across the entire retail product and service cycle, firm manufacturing to post-sale customer service interactions. Hence, retailers can use (AI) to its fullest potential will be also to influence purchases in the moment and anticipate future purchases, guiding shoppers towards the right products in a regular and highly personalized manner.

3. (AI) technology can rise the conscious customers. Customers are demanding an increased interest in the ethical practice of the brands they buy from. Todays, customers have a well-developed sense of what is solely intended to drive sales. This has lead to a rise in consumers ho make

values based judgements about what to buy and where to shop. These consumers believe their purchase habits have an impact on the world. To win customers, retailers need have good conscious to predict consumers' desire. Future, (AI) data gather technology will be a good consumer behavior predictive tool to predict about for years will now become customer expectations and will have drastically changed the path to purchase. So, (AI) data gather tool is the predictive consumer expectations tool on every interaction, they have these brands.

4. Future (AI) can be impacted to influence consumer behaviors by its potential to free up time, enhance, quality, and enhance personalization. The industries include: Healthcare industry can apply (AI) to support diagnosis by detecting variations in patient data, early identification of potential pandemics, imaging diagnostics; automat industry can apply (AI) to autonomous fleets to ride sharing, semi-autonomous features, such as driver assist, engine monitoring and predictive, autonomous maintenance; financial service industry can apply (AI) to design the suitable personalized financial planning, fraud detection and anti-money laundering and automation of customer operation; transportation and logistics industry can apply (AI) to autonomous trucking and delivery, traffic control and reduced congestion and enhanced security; technology, media and telecommunications industry can apply (AI) to search media, and recommendation, customized content creation and personalized marketing and advertising to attract retailers to promote; retail and consumer industry can apply (AI) to design personalized production, anticipating customer demand, , inventory and delivery management; energy industry can apply (AI) to read and record smart metering , more efficient grid operation and storage and predictive maintenance; manufacturing industry can apply (AI) to enhance monitoring and auto-correction of processes, supply chain and production optimization and on-demand production.

Hence, future (AI) technology will impact consumer technology when any retailers apply it to assist its manufacturing processes or product sale or service provision processes to satisfy consumers' needs, it means that it can help any retailers to influence positive emotion to consumers in their whole sale or consumption or purchase proccesses.

5. (AI) and machine learning technologies make it possible to capture, process, and inter data on a massive scale effectively , then any human being could ever do. For example, Criteo's creative technology " Kinetic design" can apply insights from 1.2 billion monthly impressions to select

and optimize individual branded advertisements components according to each shopper's preference and intent. This ensures more personalization and visually inspiring on brand ads. resulting in up to 12% more sales for (AI) technology advertiser clients.

Moreover, advertisers can now engage and inspire shoppers on a more personal level, rendering custom ads. it real-time for every impression. So, designer continues to learn from each design's success to make ads. more and more effective over time. Furthermore, brands are increasingly using paid search on retail sites to draw attention to their products on the crowded online shelf, e.g. Google shopping is a key growth area's more users are engaging with shopping ads. and across the globe. Google shopping has become essential to retailers' marketing strategies, but is a difficult channel to apply its tool to be promoted effectively . Thus, future (AI) and machine -learning technologies can dramatically improve digital commerce performance application to apply (AI) and machine learning to digital consumer. So, future (AI) technology can be applied to digital commerce aspect, it will fall into the categories of pattern recognition, classification, prediction and consumer behavior.

In conclusion, the benefits of using (AI) in digital commerce include: improved efficiency in discovering the relationships between datasets over traditional methods, which require complex modeling and coding, improved accuracy for clearly defined processes that involve a lot of manual processing, ability to deal with a large emotion of data with many attributes, for example: customer behavior data, multichannel and multi-device data , complex product data and fraud detection, more accurate analysis, such as customer segmentation sentiment, analysis and personalization frequent algorithum refreshes, such as several times a day, to capture the changes in customer and market behavior.

Finally, however, a lot of types predictive consumption behavior around (AI), in particulars that driven by vendors claiming their solutions are (AI) , ready and can deliver dramatic improvements over existing technologies. Application leaders for digital commerce can be misled into believing that (AI) can solve all their problems, which is not true for n in-depth discussion of the (AI) consumers and market behavioral predictive tool and machine -learning technologies bot. Thus, (AI) prediction consumer behavioral technology can give beneficial quantitative analysis for forecasting in business and market especially in consumer behavior and in the consumer decision-making process (consumer choice model) more effectively and efficiently.

CHAPTER THREE

Factors limit Artificial Intelligent can be the most effective and accurate consumer behavioral tool

Is (AI) the best and the most effective and accurate consumer behavioral prediction tool to compare other kinds of consumer behavioral prediction tools? Nowadays, retailing competitions are serious businessmen often find different kinds of methods to attempt to predict consumer changes. The consumer behavioral predictive methods can include as these below methods, instead of (AI) big data gathering tool.

Firstly, statistics is the popular mathematic method, it applies auto-regression, liner regression, structural equation modelling, logistic regression statistic techniques to be used to predict consumer behaviors. Secondly, it is classification method, it sis a support vector machine to assist businessmen to make consumer behavioral prediction, it also includes decision making tress diagram technique. Thirdly, it is rule mining method, it is algorithm, market base analytic etc. business marketing concept analytical tool, it also includes graph mining technique tool. Next, it is psychological prediction model tool, it is psychology prediction model too, it is a kind of psychological method to predict consumer behaviors. Finally, it is the most updated and potential artificial neural network (ANN) machine tool, it gathered big data, then it will carry on analyzing and applies psychological method to conclude the most accurate and reasonable solutions to give recommendation to businesses to predict when and how and why their consumer behaviors will change. So, it is one owned human mind's machine and owned psychological and analytical efforts to replace humans to make any judgement in order to make the most accurate predictive behavioral changes for consumers, instead of the traditional marketing concept and psychological and mathematic methods to predict consumer behavior, (AI) big data gathering tool will be another new tool.

What are the advantages of (AI) tool to be used to predict consumer behaviors as well as what are the different between it and other traditional consumer behavioral predictive tools? I shall explain as below:

Firstly, as above all case studies are explained to (AI) questionnaire design method benefit, I believe (AI) big data gathering tool can be applied to help human to analyze and design any the suitable valid questions to enquire any kinds of business consumers in order to gather the most meaning and useful opinions to conclude the most accurate consumer behavioral prediction for every questionnaire. So, future (AI)'s analytical effort and decision making effort most be exceed above human's judgement efforts. So, future (AI) can help human to design the most useful and meaning different kinds of valid questionnaire (survey) questions as well as assist humans to analyze and make accurate decision making and conclusions to give opinions to help businessmen to predict when consumer behaviors will change and how their consumption behaviors will change to influence their businesses in order to help them to make any efficient and effective and accurate solutions to avoid consumer number to be decreased and the most important benefit is that it can give opinions to help businessmen to explain why (what the factors) cause their consumer behaviors change suddenly. It will be human's efforts can not achieve to exceed (AI)'s efforts in the future.

Secondly, (AI) can make artificial machine judgement and analytical effort, without human misleading or unfair or unreasonable judgement. So, it can make more fair and reasonable and accurate conclusion to give opinions to predict when, how and why consumer behaviors will change suddenly to the kind of business in customer model building process and evaluating the results of customer relationship management –related investment more accurate.

Furthermore, (AI) big data gathering tool will help businesses to improve the success rate of acquiring customers, increasing sales and establishing competitiveness. (AI) big data gathering tool can give opinions how to build customer loyalty to be positive emotion impact and it can find solutions to avoid every client's negative emotion causes to bring complaints behavior to the businessman's product or service. For example, Telecom industry and aggressive research has been conducted in this by applying various data mining techniques to avoid long distance phone call users' complaints. If gathered any long distance phone call users' past complaint data to record what are their general complaint issues. Then, (AI) tool will analyze all these past complaint issues to conclude and give opinions to let Telecom knows whether which aspects encounter challenge that Telecom needs to improve it's long distance phone call services or functions in order to satisfy Telecom's long distance phone call users' needs for long term. After Telecom attempted to improve its services and/ or functions from (AI) opinions and solution methods, when it fell it's long distance phone call users have positive emotions to satisfy its service performance and function performance. Then, it can prove (AI) tool's opinions and solutions are useful. The consequence is that their complain numbers will be decreased and they won't plan to choose another long distance phone call telephone service company to replace Telecom long distance phone call service more easily.

So, (AI) big data gathering tool can concentrate on finding focus on components of customer relationship management method and datasets more accurate and efficient and effective than human's data gathering and analytical effort. It implies (AI) big data gathering tool has unique more efficient and effective and accurate dataset gathering and analytical and judgement and decision making effort, it is human can not achieve.

Thirdly, (AI) big data gathering tool has much customer loyalty predictive effort. It's effort is more easily subsequently selected, reviewed and classified to compare human's gathering data effort in whole data gathering and analytical process.

In (AI) big data gathering process, (AI) can organize whole big data gathering process and technique more easily in short time. It will include these four steps. The first stage is that customer identification stage, customer identification also known as acquisition has to do with targeting the population , who are most likely to become customer segmentation. So, (AI) can help different kinds of businesses to gather their competitors' consumer purchase behavior data in short time, it is human can not achieve. The second stage is that customer attraction stage, after (AI) maker has been segmented for the business when it has ensured to gather the businessman's global competitors' consumers data. Then it analyze these all data to find solutions / methods to give the best opinions to the organizations how to achieve the direct effort and resources into attracting the target customer segments. The third stage is that customer retention, it can be defined as the activity that an organization undertakes in order to reduce customer defections. TO be successful, customer retention starts with the first contact on organization has with a customer and continues throughout the entire lifetime of a relationship involves loyalty programs, one to one marketing and complaints management. SO, (AI) can consist the business to find the best or the most reasonable , efficient , effective solutions or methods and it will conclude all these solutions to find the most reasonable and useful opinions to achieve to the aim to help the business to reduce customer complain numbers and help the business to build confident loyalty relationship between it and its clients. SO, (AI)'s analytical effort and decision making effort can be more accurate than human's analytical effort and decision making effort. IT can achieve it's consumer behavioral predictive aim more accurate and efficient and effective in the shortest time to compare human.

Fourthly, (AI) big data gathering tool can design more accurate dataset program for questionnaire (survey) to compare human's questionnaire (survey) effort. It means that (AI) can spend less time to research and make judgement what are the most reasonable and meaning questions for different kinds of businesses' needs. This includes data conduction a questionnaire, survey or interview of the individual or environment researched, public data repository: This includes commercially available public data; organizational data; this contains data collected from an organizational database, organizational information system. For example, their website log details etc. It also includes company transactional data, data purchased from a company.

For example, one vehicle sale company expects to research all global vehicle sale companies' past the different kinds of vehicle styles, design sale number data, the different kinds of vehicle style, design sale price data, every country's vehicle consumer number to the vehicle purchase number data to the vehicle company in short time. (AI) big data gathering tool can help the vehicle sale company to gather all any one for these global vehicle sale competitors' past data in the short time. It is human effort, who can not achieve this efficient, effective and accurate data gathering aim for this vehicle sale company. Even, when (AI) had gathered all global it's vehicle competitors' past sale data, (AI) can make more accurate analytical and judgement and decision making effort to design different kinds of questionnaire (survey) questions to prepare to enquire it's different target segmentation vehicle potential clients in order to predict what are their needs to choose to buy any vehicles from the vehicle company. SO, (AI) tool can conclude more accurate conclusions and give the most reasonable and useful opinions to let the vehicle company to know in order to predict what are it's potential vehicle buyer's needs and manufacture the suitable vehicle styles or designs to raise their vehicle purchase desires.

Fifthly, (AI) tool is only one perfect tool for big data gathering in order to achieve accurate results and increased profit. What is (AI) big data gathering mean? The term " big data"gathering describes the accumulation and analytical of vast amounts of information, but big data is much more than a big amount of data. It is also the ability to extract meaning to sort through big volumes of numbers and find the hidden patterns, unexpected correlations and surprising connections that can be used in different industries like medical field, security and protection field or marketing that adopt " big data driven" decision making enjoy significantly greater productivity than those that do not. So, the benefits of (AI) is given to the company by using big data repaid complexity of implementation projects and hence project risks, when accelerating time to value. It is why that human's gathering effort can not replace (A I) data gathering effort.

All analysing above benefits to (AI) big data benefits to any organizations, it brinfs this question: How can (AI)apply big data gathering and analyzing to predict when and how any why consumer behavior will change suddenly? The purchase decision making process is consumers reducing purchase choice behaviors.

Consumers are being considered pure rational beings (consumer tried only to satisfy self-interest). Hence, due to future (AI) owns human's psychological , analytical , emotional predictive, purchasing decision making effort.

(A I) will be assumed to sees one customer how who will make purchase decisions. So, after the (AI) gathered all data concerns the tind of business's past customer segmentation purchase activities, e.g. age, sex,. Income level, the product's style sale number, the product price variable sale etc. different kinds complex data.

It can makemore accurate psychological and analytical effort to predict when the business's consumer behaviors will change as behaviors will change as well as find what reasons their consumption behaviors will change and how trend of their consumer behaviors will change more accurate. For example, today there are a lot of industries that use big data: healthcare (treatment) becoming personalized and patient centric and predictive analysis are used to prevent diseases for example Angelina Jolie underevent a predictive double mastectomy after learning she had 87% rich to developing breast cancer, sports (by using sensors data are collected from players during a game in order to improve their playing schemes), weather(more than 60 years of global weather analysis are used to predict the risk of future extreme events), logistics (smart tucks and smart species, agriculture (monitoring weather and soil conditions for optimum point of harvesting).

Consequently, due to the evolving consumer demands, and the ever growing digitization, the world is digitally transforming which means the new technologies are needed to be used and driven significant business improvement. So, such as why (AI) tool will be our future main predictive tool to help businesses to predict when, how and why their potential customer behavioral will change. Big data is one of the our channels through digital transformation is made, together with cloud, mobile and networks. The challenges for digital transforming and therefore using A I big data gathering tool as main technology are: digital proficiency, legacy systems, security and jobs becoming absolute.

In the future, big data can use data from text to picture , sounds, movies, musics satellite coordinates or any other type of input or output data that type of input or uouput data that came from different influential aspect. It is cloud solutions, bring big data will be for predict insight driven by business stategy, new product strategies and new consumer relationship, predictive consumer behavioral strategy. Using the right data in the right business decision will mean smart decisions, new opportunitites and utimately a big competitive advantage.Hence (AI) big data gathering tool is different is that (AI) can be one depth in-memeory database function, it can make real-time data analytics that provide meaningful information in short time, it is also the visualization tool , such as SAP Lumira, allow this exploration and understanding of the data, and ultimately supports the decision making process. All above these features, which will be human's data gathering effort who won't exceed (AI) big data gathering effort. Hence, future big data gathering will be the most main influential factors to influence robots continue develop.

CHAPTER FOUR

Limiting robots bring advantages to change market development

Airport robotic service improvement method
Any organizations will have life cycle stage from birth, growth , mature to decline. In airport service organizations have theis life cycle stages in service aspect. Airports organizatins aim to provide safe, comfortable , even shopping environment to let passengers to stay and to wait to transfer another air planes to visit another destination or arrive the country's airport to check out or check in to enter the airport to leave. If airports have life cycle stages, what the characteristics to every stage? How to improve airport service in order to reach mature life cycle stage rapidly? How to implement airport service strategy in order to reach mature life cycle stage to the aorport organization rapidly?I shall explain as below:
Any airports need to be planned in order to raise excellent service to let passengers to let any travelers choose to travel the country whether the country can provide excellent service and facilities. It will bring indirect emotion impact to influence the travelers chooce to revisit the country to travel again. However, soft or hard element or) staff service performance or airport facility), they will influence whether the different countries travelers to choose to travel to re-visit the country again. So, learning how to keep the mature or airport service life cycle stage to stay long time, it will be one important factor to influence any airport business in success.
In the birth life style stage to airport, airport organizations must maintain the capability to provide expert advice to airport owners an matters

including operational safety, during construction, environmental compatibility, and airport development standards. No other private or public organization can be expected maintain this level of proficiency. These value-added services enhance public trust when assuring consistant application of standards for the nation's airport system. So, it seems that when the new airport is built if it hopes its passenger customers can consider themselves emotion need. So, it ought concentrate on nowadays airplane landing cunways or airport transfer free service transport etc. facilities can let them to feel safe when they were walking in any airport places. If they feel anywhere are dangerous when they are walking or staying in the ne sirport, then new airport non safe or dangerous factor may influence travelers to choose the country to travel again.

Any new airports will need have good new national airport plan in order to it might operate in the near future with respect to safety areas. The plan elements may include as below:

Achieving zero accidents aim, establish standard safety areas at all commercial service airports , achieving the most minimum 85% of all passenger flights operate on runways with safe feeling, increase measure to 100% of all passenger flight operating on runways with standard safety areas after three months. Within 5 years, 95% of all passenger flights begin and end on runways with standard safety areas.

On benefits aspect, aims to mobilize work force to improve safety area performance describes realistic investment benefits. So, in any new airports birth life cycle stage, they must need to consider safety and expenditure for repair aspect in order to keep its service performance to avoid passengers have dissatisfactory feeling when they are staying in their new airports.

When the country has many travelers travel to the country , then the country's new airport passengers number must increase. It is its the new airport growth life cycle stage. These are critical success factors influence the airport, whether it can improve service performance in order to excite different countries travelers visiting the country's airport desire or grow up the visitors number successfully. The critical success factors may include: Having necessary support from internal and externa stakeholders to implement and willing to share information and identify anywhere the total airport facilities of repair needs that are both reliable and feasible projections to let passengers to feel more safe feeling when they are staying in the airport, understand its future service vision and mission, set strategic direction and goals to process/product specific objectives and decision-making across and doen the organization, define, model and prioritize planning prcesses critical for mission performance, practice hand-on sernior management ownership of planning process and allow field, personnel flexiblity in performing jobs, adjust organizational structures , an essessment program to evaluate planning process and product management , e.g. national airport system performance, create organizational understanding of the value management to customer and stakeholder current and future expectations developing human resources management strategies to support new process that solves needs planners and engineers, building information resources strategies change, especially for entering data at the source and maintains data integrity and timeliness.,establish central support group to support reengineering efforts, outreach and training efforts across the organization, phase in short-and long-term results that achieve set goals and objectives over the next two years.

Thus, when one new airport begins to feel passengers number is increasing. It ought experience the growth life cycle stage to the new airport , if it hopes that it can reach mature life cycle stage rapidly as well as keeps its mature life cycle stage to stay in this stage long time or reachs the airport service performance to the most satisfactory level in this mature life cycle stage. It must need to attempt to plan these strategies to implement in order to avoid decline life cycle stage occurs in short time. So, it explains why some new airport can experience the development to mature life cycle stage from grow life cycle stage in short time,even when it reachs mature life cycle stage. It can keep to stay in this stage long time. The reason is that it had prepared effective strategies to achieve how to improve its airport service performance aim in order to satisfy passenger needs. When they are staying in the country's airport any time. Hence, every year revising service performance is needed to any airports.

Any airports must have development processes. The question is that whether the airport needs how long time to reach growth or mature life cycle stage from birth stage or decline life cycle stage will be delayed how long to occur. The development processes may mean that the airport development life cycle stages changes that had toard a particular result or even as a series of continuous actions or operations coducting to an end (Merriam-Webster, 2013).

reference

Merriam-webster (2013). On line dictionary. Available at:
https://www.merriam-webster. com/(last accessed July , 8 2013).

Hence, any airport organizations with experience development pricess. When the new airport is built, it must be in the birth life cycle stage. Its passengers number can not increase rapidly. It needs time to grow their number. But, when the new airport operates a period, many different countries begin feel this new airport is existence in the country. They will attempt to catch airplance to visit this country airport to catch airplane to visit tis country airport to travel. If they feel this country airport service performance can satisfy their short time staying feeling or its passengers or airports visitors number may increase rapidly. It meand that this airport is experiencing growth life cycle stage. So, if the airport can attract many visitors in short time. It will reduce time to growth life cycle stage from birth life cycke stage.

So , service performance may be one important factor to inflow the airport grows. When the airport develops to the period, passengers number can not increase rapidly, it may be the airport's mature life cycle stage. Due to it's passengers number can not grow rapidly, its passengers number also may reduce. When its passengers number has significant decrease, if its reduction number is increasing more. It implies that the airport is experiencing decline life cycle stage. All any country's airport may experience whole life cycle stages. If the country's airport can not implement successful strategies, it may experience birht life cycle stage in long time because it can not grow its passengers number significantly. So, any airports need to learn how to help them to change growth life cycle stage, even mature life cycle stage can stay in long time easily. If they hope to attract many different countries passengers to visit their airports or travel themselves countries or enjoy to stay short time in themselves airports in order to grow themselves airline industry development.

- How can robotic service management method can improve airport service performance?

Overall processes in an airport may involve passengers, luggage, cargo, aircraft movements, ground handling, and crews . All of these operations can be systematised into processes at airport terminal. Three main types of processes can be established departing , arrival and transfer . Departure consists in catching a flight to a final or intermediate destination, arrival consists in landing and leaving the airport, and transfer consists in landing at the airport only to catch another flight to a final or an intermediate destination. Airports also deal with cargo. It involves in the movement of cargo by air, cargo fies from the shopper to the consignee through one or more airlines. However, when the airport can let them freight forwarder, being familiar with the necessary procedures how permits the airline to concentrate on the provision of air transport and to avoid time consuming details of the facilitation and landside distribution system. It will raise efficiency and improve service performance. The services product by the ground handling are crucial to the success and efficiency of the airport operations.

These services are usually provided by specialised companies. Briefly, it includes the luggage treatment, passengers carrying from plan to terminal when needed and aircraft assistance. Also, focusing on crew, there are two majoe processes, one for departures and the other for arrivals. The crew members also have to pass the security and passport controls. However, they have special channels for this. Once they reach the aircraft, the similarities with the passengers‘ procedure stop. Hence, they have to perform a set of activities , such as check the aircraft load sheets and help passengers to name a few. Also airport terminal operations processes for passengers and luggage, typically for departures , passengers do the check on the airline area, pass security controls, proceed to the general lounge and lastly to the gate holding area. arriving passengers are able to immediately go from the luggage claim area, but the non-passengers have to pass the passport control at first. After this passengers have to decide if they need to declare goods or not as the paths are different . Hence, if the airport can reduce all of this service processes are less complex as immigration check in-out service, liggage claim can be efficient to carry when passengers need to find themselves luggage. Then, it will reduce waste time and let they satisfy airport service absolutely. So, reducing service process time amy also help the airport to increase customers number significantly. When airport role is the middleman between airlines , cargo transport service providers and passengers, e.g. short time transport cargo service and reducing passengers check in or check out service time. then, it will let them to feel more satisfactory service to the airport.

Hence, airport capacity is as a multifactor function leaves open the exact relationship between the factors but stresses that all factors are relevant to assess airport capacity . So , understanding airport capacity and what drives the capacity usage at airports may provide an insight in the set of instructments available to optimise the use of capacity. All of these factors may influence any capacity of an airport, they may include as below:

For example, technical constraints, e.g. ATM per hour service in a runway in a combined arrival and departure fashion, when many passengers are staying at the airport, they can withdraw money from ATM easily. So, ATM number facilities service supply number and location choice to the airport factors will infuence passengers ' satisfactory level, another factor is environmental constraints, it can directly offer the wellbeing of the communities surrounding the negative emotion to passengers and communities surrounding the airprt. For this factor, the change in technology and/or operational procedures can provide more capacity in the system.

Airline business models factor, it can affect the capacity spoke model when other under a point-point one ,these models directly affect the peak hour operational capacity, particularly in big international hubs. Airlines often compete with high frequencies between destinations, thus increasing the number of movements. In addition, conncectivity also has downsides for this model: the delays in one airport might be exported and sometimes in another, due to the connectivity influencing the real capacity. This factor has been setting economic incentives or pricing models. Furthermore, expanding information systems, from one airport to multiple airports gate-to-gate concept, and the use of larger airport to redcuce frequencies.

Hence, above these factors may influence whether the airport needs how long time to reach maturiry life cycle stage when it is staying the growth life cycle stage. It depends on how its strategies implementation and how environment influence its implementation , if it hopes to achieve to reach the maturity life cycle stage in success in short time.

Finally, I shall explain life cycle cst analysis to any country pavement strategy will bring what significant influential benefits to any airports continue to develop in order to avoid to reach decline life cycle stage time in short time easily , when they are staying in the mature life cycle stage. In the construction or rehabilitation investments of highway's pavements, it is already common to perform a life-cycle analysis or life cycle cost analysis for different alternatives to airport pavements. Becauae when any airport pavements are using for a long time, every day has many airplanes need to fly to land on the pavement. It can bring significant repace influence when the airport has many airplanes are needed to land on the pavements every day in the maturity life cycle stages.

Hence, how to evaluate the repair cost expenditure budget in order to satisfy every day air planes land on the airport pavement need. In the calculations are different cost factors (including direct and indirect cost)to any airport itself pavement. Direct costs are related to the critical construction cost landing on pavement activities and are calculated with information from the airport agency and constructors that work for them. The indirect costs are related with the loss of daily revenue of the airport during work activities, such as landing on the airport pavement.

Runways are the most critical pavements area of airport , so it is critical to ensure the quality of these pavement to let airplanes to land on the airport safety, e.g. they need to be constructed with sufficient strength to carry the moving airport and have a high resistance to skidding and aquaplaining. It is most of the time accomplished with reconstructions or deep rehabilitation. Hence, predicting how much will spend on airport pavement facilities expenditure must need in every day.

However, the life cycle assessment (LCA) is a mult step procedure for calculating the life time environmental impact of a product or service is needed to any airport organizations, when they reachs maturity life cycelt stage . The complex process includes goal and cope definition in inventory analysis impact assessment. The process is vaturally iteractive as quality and completeness of information is constantly being testes. When the definition of the aim and scope of the study is done the next step is the development of an inventory, in which all significant environmental burdens during the lifetime of the product,, such as airport pavements or process , such as airplanes landing on the pavement or airplanes leaving from the pavement in the airport.

(Araujo, Oliveria & Silve) 2014 explained that life cycle snslysis of pavements are focused on the activities of extraction, production, transportation application of materials, concisely the construction of the road. Because its difficult to obtain other relevant data knowing that the use phase of the pavement is predominant with repect to energy consumption and also to gas emissions related to the atmosphere. One of the main factors for the use phase is the rolling resistance, this depends on the surface and structural characteristics of the different pavements.

reference

Araujo, J.P.C. Oliveria, J.R.M. & Silva H.M.R.D. (2011) . the importance of the use phase on the LCA of environmentally friendly solutions for asphalt road pavements. transportation research part D: trasport and environment, 32(0), 97-110. Retrieved in March 2015 from://
dx. doi.org/10.1016/j.trd.2014.07.006.

How non driving vehcile electronic vehicle how influence future global transport market developement

Nowadays, since electronic vehicle invention, it brought competition to fight traditional gas vehicle martet. Electronic vehicle is only needed to be charged battery, then battery will bring energy to push the electornic car to be driven fastly. So traditional vehicle market is experiencing decline life cycle stage. When, electronic vehicle is popular to be accepted to every drivers. In fact, when we drive cars on the roads, our cars will have gas emission to polluate our sir. Earth warmth is dramatically increasing. The main reason is that global air is polluted, e.g. frequent driving activities will bring air pollution when gas emission is caused. Hecnce, environment vehicle is only needed to charged battery. Every time battery charged can bring one day driving time power or enerty to let drivers to drive . So, basing on environmental protection and battery long time driving both reasons, it brings strengths to electronic vehicle to persuade global any drivers to choose to buy electronic vehicle more than traditional gas vehicle. I shall research these questions: These questions may concern: Will the gas vehicle be influenced to experience the decline life cycle stage rapidly when the electronic vehicle is accepted to be popular to drive ? Can traditional gas vehicle avoid decline life cycle stage comes as well as if traditional gas vehicle real prepares to experience decline life cycle stage ? Can it re-grow to change to enter growth life cycle stage again? Can new electronic vehicle market influence traditional gas vehicle market to shorten time to experience decline life cycle age rapidly?

In our driving history, cars invention had helped us do not need to spend long walking time to go to anywhere conveniently. In fact, due to technological limit, e.g. bus, taxi, tram, train must use gas to be energy to push them to be driven on the roads. When car invention period, or it may call car market birth life cycle stage period. In the 1800 year beginning , human does not know what car function or why we need car. When cars had been invented, it is global whole car industry borth life cycle stage period. This period its characteristics are: In societies , people accepted car tools to drive on the roads. Many people feel to spend money to buy cars, it is waste money, because they may choose to catch any kinds of public transport tools, e.g. bus, train, tram, taxi, ferry, undergroundtrain to arrive any destinations conveniently. So, from 1800 year to 1900 year, global whole car industy had been still keeping in the growth life cycle stage.

Because in global society, many people hasd been general accepting public tranposrt tools, their fee are vey cheap and passengers can spend short time to catch them to go to anywhere, they can provide long transport service time for office working people, student from morning to evening time. Hence, this 100 years period, global car sale number could not significant increase, because public transport tools could bring convenience to any one when they needed to leave homes to arrive far away destination in short time.

Hence, global car industry ought not develop rapidly, because many peoplecould not accept to spend money to buy cars to replace to catch any public transport tools. But after 1900 year, global whole gas vehicle industry began to experience growth life cycle stage. Because global many people had jobs to do, unemployment ratio begain to reduce. In society, rich people number began to increase. It based on theseboth factors: families began to consider to attempt to buy any kinds of cars in order to attempt to buy any kinds of cars in order to let them to feel enjoyable to drive to go to anywhere. So, from 1901 year to 2000 year, it may be global whole gas vehicle market growth life cycle stage . In this period, global car buyers number had been increasing significantly . In average, global every family may own at least one car, even more. It depends on whether how many members number, the family has and whether the family has how many member(s), he/she has own one car licence. Moreover, in society, many people began to accept second hand cars, because second hand cars must be chaper to compare new cars as well as it is real one good choice for the low income car buyer social consumer groups in society. So, in this global vehicle market growth life cycle stage, instead of new car buyers number had been increasing significantly, the second hand car buyers number had also been increasing significantly in the same time. So, global new cars and secod hand car buyers number had increased rapidly every year, because global population is increasing. It also caused many working people did not like to spend long time to queue to wait public transport tools, it is another factor to persuade people chooce to buy cars to drive to go to offices or schools or anywhere in their relax time, e.g. holiday, sunday. So, this 100 year, may be global whole car industry growth life car cycle stage.

After 2000, it may be global car industy mature life cycle ctage , many car manufacturers begun to innovate any kinds of traditional cars to change to advanced engine function, auto-window, auto dooe functions , navigation road locaion search function, even non-manual driven artificial intelligent car invention. So, after 2000 year, due to global car buyers begun to pursue comfortable drivin feeling. They need to pursue comfortable driving feeling. They need to buy unique design of cars, or more functions of cars to drive on the road . Hence, global different unique function and styles of cars purchase needs had been significant increasing. Moreover, car prices had also been increasing more, due to more different unique functional and styles of car purchase needs had been increasing in order to satisfy the rich or high income car buyers group. So, after 2000, it may be global car market 's mature life cycle stage.

But, I believe that global car market's mature life cycle stage can not keep long time. The main reason is because the electronic car invention. After 2000 year, since one kind of new transport tool of electronic car invention, it influences many gas car owners or non car owners feel interesting to learn how to drive electronic cars and feel whether what advantages that electronic cars can satisfy their driving needs. IN special, environmental protection awareness drivers must believe electornic cars can reduce air pollution when they choose to drive them on the roads , due to none gas emission effect to pollute our earth air. When they choose to drive electronic cars, due to they only need to charge battery, then their electronic cars can be driven on the roads in short time rapidly. Even, report also indicated driving electronic cars accident occurrence chance may be also influenced to reduce to compare driving gas cars usually. So, electronic vehicle market may be future main competitor to global traditional gas vehicle market.

May electronic vehicle invention influence future gas vehicle shorten time to experience to decline life cycle stage rapidly? How gas vehicle market may avoid the shorten time to experience decline life cycle stage if electronic vehicle market may influence its development in global car manufacture industry? I shall attempt to solve these challenges as below:

IN fact, electronic vehicle innovation is not long time , so the global electronic vehicle manufacturing and sale market is experiencing birth life cycle stage. Can electronic vehicle market reduce to shorten time to experience growth, even mature life cycle stages. It depends on these factors:

The factors may affect battery electronic vehicle energy consumption and driving behavior impact. They may include whether environment protection awareness will increase or decrease to global nay one gas car owners or non car owners. Because if global environment protection awareness increase, it will influence gas car owners or non car owners (potential either battery electronic vehicle energy or gas vehicle energy car choice buyers), begun to feel their frequent driving gas vehicle behaviors may bring air pollution or global warming, temperature rises weather disaster occurrence in the future. They alsoknow battery electronic vehicle energy consumption price may be cheap to same to gas vehicle energy consumption. Moreover, they may feel that if they change to drive battery electronic vehicles, it may help them to minimize environmental air pollution impacts of the end of life stage and brings positive impacts on improving climate change and air quality for our future. So, if many car owners or non car owners feel that they have responsibility to protect our climate environment pollution. Then, battery electronic vehicle buyers number will have possible to increase rapidly in short time. Due to the significant impact of gas vehicle and battery electronic vehicle their life cycle analysis can be utilized to analyze the advantages and disadvantages to cause car buyers make comparison between them and gas vehcile and battery electronic vehcile both kinds vehicles are highly complex supply chain choice in the automobile industry nowadays. Moreover, due to carbon intensity of this stage was calculated from emission factors at the global car manufacture industry. Hence, emission factor may be one important influential factor to influence any one makes car purchase decision or either gas or battery electronic car purchase decison.

For example , in our societies, if many peopl own environment protection awareness, then global gas vehicle buyers number may be influenced to reduce, even the owning gas vehicle families may be influenced to choose to buy battery electronic cars to replace their gas cars. They may sell their gas vehicles to any one, even to steel manufacturers easily. Hence, gas vehicle on steel existence number may also reduce ot they can disappear in our road in short time rapidly. If batttery electronic vehcile can be popular to accept to drive on the road to any one driver in our societies. Then, battery electronic cars may be influenced to increase driving needs to any one driver. it's sale number may also influenced to increase rapidly. Consequently, it may have chance to experience to growth life cycle stage from birth life cycle stage in short time rapidly in global whole electronic car manufacturer and sale market.

Then another influential factor concerns how owning car consumers feel the charge of the battery energy use of resources in comparison to conventional gas energy use of resources to driving cars. In combination with the regional electricity mix these factors influence the energy materials for a specific car market. For these first life cycle phases a range of values is possible to battery electronic car market. If in our societies, there are many people choose to use battery charge energy resource to drive electronic cars, their prices are very reasonable to compare gas vehicles or they feel gas will face rapid shortage challenge, if global any one only likes to drive gas vehicle. Then, they may be influenced to choose to buy the battery electronic vehicles to replace gas vehicles. Hence, enery resource used to car my also be one main factor to influence any one car buyer individual either battery electronic car or gas vehicle purchase choice.

Hence, it implies that the life style environmental impacts and energy resource used both impacts of battery electronic cars are a topic of increasing relative importance of the vehicle production stage and the maximum impact on climate change (ingc02/km) that is observed by many climate scientists, their observation to climate change good or bad change effect may influence global battery electronic vehicle needs. So, how clean are battery electric cars, it will be one popular topic for environmental scientists to environmental protection awareness car owners and non car owners. T o analysis hoe to cause electric car life cycle changes. The arrival of the electric car has brought with it an array of life cycle factors that influence the carbon emission level to any one country's environment.

Influence of national electricity grid over the use phase, so it implies that if the country feels carbon emission level is high , due to gas vehicle may bring carbon emission to pollute air to the country. Although, factory's carbon emission or airplane carbon emisson may be one factor to influence the country's air pollution level to be increase. The year has high carbon emission level, it considers gas vehicle air carbon emission level whether it is high or low in the year. So, if the country's gas vehicle car owners number is sudden increasing rapidly. Consequently, it will evaluate that the car increasing number may influence the country itself carbon emission level to be high and it may cause air pollution seriously.

Hence, battery electric car industry life cycle whether when it can experience growth life cycle stage or mature life cycle stage from birth life cycle stage, it depends on what carbon emisson level to any one country. If this year has many countries believe their high carbon emissin level is due to gas vehicle 's carbon emission causes. Then, this high carbon emission level report factor may raise many car owners or non car owners consider environment protection awareness and it may also influence many car buyers choose to buy battery electric cars to replace gas cars to drive on the road frequently in this year.

Also in order to avoid themselves countries' air pollution is more serious. Hence, global carbon emission rise or fall level and any one environmental protection awareness psychological both factors may influence future battery electric car market development. They may have close relationship to influence any one traditional gas vehicle owner to buy one new battery vehicle vehicle to replace it to drive on the road, or any one potential car purchaser makes final battery electric car or gas vehicle decision absolutely.

On conclusion, above these factors may explain whether it is possible that battery electronic vehicle invention may influence future gas vehicle market changes to decline life cysle stage from mature life cycle stage. It depends on whether environmental protection awareness to car owners increasing or decreasing number , carbon emission level whether it is high or low, gas energy resource facing shortage factors to influence future electronic vehicle need.

Management science solves public transport passenger queue problem

Waiting Line (Queuing) Models: solution imbalanced taxi and passenger queue in urban public transportation service case

The Four Problems Of Urban Transportation (And The Four Solutions)

The fixed-route bus and the bicycle solve at least one urban problem better than new technologies urban transportation problem case. There are four main problems in urban transportation that require four separate solutions. Some urban transportation design recommendion argued that technology can solve some problems, but not the same problem that public transit solves."The city has four separate problems of urban transportation which have four separate kinds of solutions, and it is very important to not mistake the solution for one problem for the solution for a different problem."

The first solution :

Bus stop time real -time information technology and apps solution method

Friction arises between a transit system and its users when the users don't have the information they need when they need it. That problem has been largely solved, Walker said, by information technology and apps. "That has been a fantastic transformation. Some of you may not be old enough to remember what life was like without real-time information, when you just went right out into the snow and wondered when the bus was coming."

The second solution:

Innovation method

The innovation method solves the city has four separate problems of urban transportation may include: Emissions and Energy Efficiency: "for which we're currently working on electric vehicles, and that's fantastic." Labor and Safety: The cost of labor is the primary driver of operation costs for passenger transport, Walker said. "It is why your bus doesn't come more often, and it is also why Uber can't make money." Autonomous vehicles will address that and the accident rate. "There is a problem with the efficient use of labor, and also a colossal problem of safety for which we are talking about autonomous vehicles, and that's fantastic." Space: "And there is a fourth problem which is the efficient use of space, for which the solution is on the one hand, cycling and walking, and on the other, public transit provided by big vehicles."

The third soution:

The fixed-route bus or train solutione method is the best solution reason

The fixed-route bus or train is the vehicle of the future, because it remains the most efficient way to move large numbers of people through the congested space of a city. In his critique of public transit, Musk pointed out that people prefer "individualized transport, that goes where you want, when you want," like the Tesla Model S. But Walker contends individualized transport that goes where you want when you want can't move people through a congested city as efficiently as a fixed-route bus.

"We are always going to need vehicles sized to the appropriate capacity requirement, which means big buses in big cities," he said. "Our friends in the tech industry, including many of you here, and I love what you're doing, are always trying to sell us stories about how everything will fit together into a magnificent fusion. They want us to mix it up, to think about how it combines. And I'm always saying, but wait a minute, if you're going to be a smart customer you have to think about how they work separately as well."

Skills shortages on developing country market

Future developing countries need to develop their economy, so they need to employ many employees who own technical skills and /or soft skills. What kind of technical skills and/or soft skills , the developing countries' employees who will need to order to raise competition in local job market ? I shall indicate the developing country China example. China is one developing country, employers will need different kinds of skillful labors to assist them to develop their businesses. However, China employers will face skillful labour shortage challenge. Although Chinese young age population is high, but many of them do not to be encouraged to learn enough skillful knowledge to fill future new skillful positions. So, the fast speed of training will be important to influence China supply and demand labour market to be more accurately as well as future China's the quality of labour demand number will be influenced to be raised after they have enough training to learn new skills.

How to solve future China skillful shortage of labour? Firstly, nowadays, China employers need to teach their employees to learn how to use and how to operate robotic skills in China's factories. AI robotic has been early developing, so they need to prepare to learn robotic management and operating technical and soft skills in order to satisfy future China factory automation industry development.

China is one world's factory for low-end products to high quality information products, high end technology and services. So, China will need many high skilled workers to assist manufacturers to manufacture many different kinds of products to export or local sale. Moreover, robotic manufacturing skillful workers will also need because robotic will be accepted to assist manual workers to work in China's any factories. This has led to greater demand for labour with upgraded skills and competence. So, it seems that China's workers need to learn any high technological manufacturing knowledge, e.g. learning how to co-operate with robotics to raise productive efficiencies, which will be future many China's manufacturers‘ skills need intention.

So, when any one of China manufacturer invests robotics to work in its factory . Then, the China manufacturer's labours ought need to know how to co-operate with the robotics to raise productivities and efficiencies. Moreover, these China service industries, e.g. IT, software, accounting, finance, marketing and customer service management, e.g. waiter, property security, shopping center customer service etc. service occupations. In the future, robotics can also used to participate any one of these service industries' part of tasks in order to raise service performance. So, any one of these service industries‘ employees need to learn how to operate with robotics in order to achieve the most excellent service performances to satisfy consumers' needs. So, China service industries labours ought need to learn how to co-operate or manage service natural robotics to work together more efficiently because future China manufacturers will prefer to employ the labours who know how to co-operate and manage and control any service natural robotics more easily and efficiently in order to achieve the most excellent service performance to satisfy customers needs.

Hence, it seems that China manufacturing and service workers need to spend time and effort to learn how to co-operate with manufacturing natural robotics to manufacture any products in factories efficiently or deliver any cargos in warehouses more efficiently or serve customers to let them to feel excellent service performance in restaurants or shopping centers or properties or offices receiption counters. Then, when their China employers apply robotics to participate to work in factories, restaurants, shopping centers, cinemas, offices or properties reception etc. different working places . These low skillful labours will be dismissed easily, due to robotics can replace them to manufacture any products or provide services to satisfy clients' needs in order to let them to fell robotics' performances are more excellent to compare human service labours or their productive efficiencies are more effort to compare workers. So, future China workers need to learn how to cooperate or manage or contol with robotics to work more efficiently, if they do not expect to be dismissed easily.

In the future several occupations have been identified as the most frequent movers between all labour market states. The elementary occupations include: waiters, bar staffs, clearners, catering assistants, construction and security service workers, care workers, sales assistants and general clerks etc. So, the low educational level workers can learn these soft wkills to raise whose professional workering level to prepare to do these above positions in global elementary occupation job market.

The changes of employer were most frequent for IT programmers, doctors, electricians, carpenters, skilled workers in global labour market. These skilled occupations will have manpower shortage supply challenge, due to either people feel the educatonal level is under low. So, there has no many people have interest to know these knowledg to prepare their elementary careers. So, these kinds of low skilled occupations will have not enough human power supply to global labour job market also, the high skilled or educational job support.

Moreover, the high skilled occupations also encounter labour shortage issue. The skills in short supply related to experienced canadidates e.g. five years or more. For example, pharmaceutical , biogharma and food innovation industries. The occupational shortage roles include: Chemists, analytical scientists, product formulation, analytical development for roles in biopharma, quality control analyst includes pharmaco-vigilance, i.e. drug safety roles. The demand for engineering industry aspect which will aos increase the labour shortage includes process and design (research and development, quality control, automation, lean processes) are skillful labours need to help employers to achieve these intentions. They may include raising competitiveness, boosting productivity and skills availability. So, if future these above any one of occupation labours can not achieve these benefits to satisfy their employers' needs. Then, his/her average weekly or hourly wages will be reduced. It means that the unskilled labour under skilled labour wage can not increased more easily, even they own many year working experiences in any one of above these occupations. If the employer feels the labour is unskilled or below skilled level for any one of these occupations in these any one industry aspect, e.g. wholesale and retal , human health, education, accomodaton and food , construction, professional activities, financial service , public administration, and defence, transportation etc. occupations. Then, these industries' unskilled or below skilled level workers' salaries will be lower level to compare the higher skilled workers who work in any one of these industries.

The reason why future employers need to employ skilled labours. One explanation for slow recovery in demand in negative impact on investment is a prolonged period of high unemployment. This is led to job weekers left labour market or became unemployable due. So, future low skillful level will be one important factor to cause unemployment in society as well as nowadays labours ought need consider whether their skills are needed to improve in order to avoid future competition in job market.

2.1 Why do future labours need to learn worldwide readiness skills

Future employers need employees own worldwide readiness skills, such as reading , writing and arithmatic. Why do employees need worldwide readiness skills? In the future, high economic growth countries need high wage positions, high opportunity jobs which need a large number of skills required of job candidates of these positions " job readinss" and not " job training" , which support developments of these importance and widely desired skills won't only support the success to high-opportunity positions, but also be developed for future success in the competitive global economy. Because real-time business intelligence is needed for the talent marketplace to employ talent employees. So, it explains that it will have many future employers hope to employ owning readiness skillful employees to help them to develop their businesse intelligently. Hence, present employees ought need to hard to train readiness skills to prepare whose future employers' job requirements in the future competitive global job market.

2.2 Why these occupations need readiness skills

In the future these occupations will need to raise readiness skills. For example, mathematical science, teachers (post-secondary), management analysts, computer and information systems, managers, first-line supervisors of construction traders, solar photovoltaic installers. All of these occupations , employers need staffs to own good readiness analytic ability to help them to do more accurate real-time business intelligent decisions. The representative occupations include oral and written communication skills, project management, teamwork, marketing and creativity . Moreover, they need to own specific technology skill, deep science and math or even most business skills as well as these skills are "soft" skills more than hard skills. These kinds of occupation employees need own cooperative effort, creativity, problem solving, detail orientation and integrity personal characteristics, which are relevant across all knowledge and domains.

Therefore, in the future, science, technology,engineering and mathematics relevant occupations need to own more read and analytic skills more than other kinds of occupations. Because these organizations need those professionals on knowledge acquisition, literacy analysis, synthesis and critical thinking skills that will impact their organizations to bring more critical thinking beneficial team culture. These occupational top skills will include oral and written communication skills, project management skill, team oriented skill, marketing and creativity skills, problem solving skill, detail oriented skill, self-motivated skills, management and analytical skills, coaching skill, business process modeling skills, work independent skill, strong leadership skills, management experience and business requirements gathering. All of these skills which will be future employers who need to employ these kinds employees who own these skills in preference. Also, all of these skills concentrate on soft skills more than hard skills. It seems that when above occupational applicants who own any one of these skills, even more than one skills. Then, he/she will have more chance to be selected to employ. Also occupation specific skills requirements are more needed to compare cross-functional skills for above of any one occupation. Because the high concentration of cross-functional skills require " job readiness" and not " job training" for success, e.g. communication, integration and presentation skills, entrepreneurialism and related skills, microsoft office software skills.

Of particular interest is communication, integration and presentation skills. These skills include ability to seek, evaluate and examine information and data create a reasoned position, present findings and make a case for or advocate for position. So, these skills are very important and they can help future applicants who expect to win any kinds of these positions easily. However, the hard skills can help these applicants to be more successful to win any kinds of these positions when they own these hard skills, e.g. microsoft office, powerpoint, excel , word, microsoft project etc. softwares. In conclusion, the global economy is dynamic and many of the skills required for positons in the future will need good technologies and work practices to be developed. The number of skills required t be successful in the jobs forecast to be most in demand in the future is growing. So, it explains that why future any one of these occupations which will need soft skills more than hard skills, due to organizations like to employ the employees who own managerial and analytical effort more than hard skills productive effort to assist their organizations to develop more easily.

2.3 Data -analysis skill needs

In the future, most organizations will have a number of jobs that include data analysis. Economists and labor market forecasters predict occupations need data analytical skill will need much. In addition, fast technological development means th types of technologies and applications workers in this field will need to be familiar with data analytical skill rapidly. It seems that data analytical jobs will have new job opportunity to employees with in-demand skills in future global labor market.

Why and how do employers demand for data analysis skills? Data analysis skills mean the ability to gather, analyze and draw practical conclusions from data as well as communicate data findings to others. The occupations include: data analyst, data scientist, statistician, market research analyst, financial analyst,research manager. In business career, many employers expect to employ statisticans, operations research analysts, market research analysts and marketing specialists to assist their organizations to gather useful data from market in order to analyze and draw practical conclusions and finding the best solutions or methods to win their competitors.

Therefore, these data analysis jobs will have much need. Large size organizations with 500 or more employees were more likely than small or medium size organizations with 25 to 499 employees to plan hired data analysis positons in the future. For example, human source department will use big data to help make strategic decisions. How HR uses big data . HR will use big data for sourcing, recruitment, or selection, identifying causes of turnover and/or employee retention strategies or trends, managing talent and performance. Why organizations do not use big data. It is possible that they lack of knowledge expertise, the majority of organizations will have data analysis positions within accounting and finance department, human resources department, business and administration department, information technology department, marketing, advertising and sales department, supply chain and operations department, research and development department, customer service department and other departments. So, future data analysis skill will need to used in different organizational departments.

However, publicly and privately owned for-profit organizations were more likely than government organizations to have data analysis positions in the marketing, advertising and sales function. Also, data analysis skills are required to different levels in any organizations , such as entry level, non-management / individual contributor level, mid-level management level, senior management or executive level. The analyst, research analyst, market research analyst, scientist-based titles include: data scientists , research scientist, scientist, other descriptive titles include researcher, statistician, mathematician and other . So, data analysis positions will have many different skills to be selected to any one data analysis professional. For example, the data analysis professional can select either to learn the ability to interpret and communicate data analysis results skill or to learn how gathering or analyzing data skill. So, data analysis skill is not only one skill, it is more than one skill to let any one employee to select to learn.

Why do organizations need data analysis professionals? On workforce planning aspect, organizations expect to let strategic direction and content of workforce needed for future business objectives easier, analyzing workforce: supply analysis, demand analysis and gap analysis more easy, developing action plan : recruiting and training plans to deal with gaps more easier, implementing action plan, monitoring, evaluating and revising plan more easier. So, organizations expect the data analysis professional can help them to solve these challenges, such as using of advanced technology solutons to integrate disparate planning sources; data availability and format; accessing to and understanding of the organization's data and analytics, developing business case to gain support from senior management and collaboration among HR staff, managers and executive easier. Future industries need data analysis professionals may include manufacturing health care and social assistance, scientific and technical service, finance and insurance, educational services , government agencies, retail trade, transportation and warehousing, construction, utilities, accommodation, and food services, waste management and remediation services, entertainment, and creation, real estate and rental and leasing , repair and maintenance, agriculture, forestry, fishing and hunting, personal and laundry services etc.

In conclusion, data analysis job need explains why future readiness and data analytical skills will be popular needed in global labour market , due to these both skills are labour shortage and employers will need employees own big data readiness and data analytical both skills in order to win whose competitors more easier.

2.4 What are regional dynamic skills of global labour market demand when robotic participate labor market

Businessmen expect to improve better economic environment, they will prefer to recruit the most sought after skills of intelligent employees to bring positive beneficial impact to organizations. However, technology and digization has had a significant influence on workers. Future globalization will trend digital economic development. Hence, it will influence workers' skills to be changed also. In fact, not all changes are positive because some workers will possible lose jobs, either due to new technology replaces their jobs or they lack enough effort to improve their skills in global digital economic labour market environment.

It brings this question: What are regional dynamic skills need with digital business environment is growing. In fact, organizations will continue to deal with skills shortages, labour markets across the global are continually changing. so, more employers and workers will need to adopt innovate working pattern, e.g. on call jobs, freelance jobs will grow popularly. The greater flexibility afforded to employ regard.

Finally, digitalisation includes artificial intelligence, big data , online platforms. All these new technology will influence future employees how to worker. For example, they can apply online platform to work at home conveniently. So, they do not need to go to offices. They can finish their jobs and send to their employers by email easily. This kinds of job pattern can raise efficiencies and employers do not need go to offices often.

An important implication of innovating working which needs the employees who own digital skills in order to serve organizations more efficiently. So, employers are increasingly able to access demographics that were hitherto less active in labour markets. For example, future more women are joining the labour market because part time and self employment opportunities make it easier. This kinds of job pattern can raise efficiencies and employees do not need go to offices often.

An important implication of innovating working which needs the employees who own digital skills in order to serve organizations more efficiently. So, employers are increasingly able to access demographic that were hitherto less active in labour markets. For example, future more women are joining the labour market because part time and self employment opportunities make it easier to manage family with work life. So, digital skilling needs will cause many women lose jobs in possible. If the women lack digital job skills. Because high digital skill occupations need, like those requiring research, medical treatment and architectural design occupational digital skills are more common in the services sector, more women who own digital skill who can compete to win.

High digital skill occupations more easier than men because employers usually select female to do high skill occupations easier than make. However, if those professional service female employees can not learn how to apply digital skills to do these researchs medical treatmentm architectural design professional service jobs. Then, it is also different for these professional service femal employees to raise competition in global labour professional service market. So, these professional service female employees need to learn how to apply digital to do themselves jobs in future global professional service labour market. Otherwise, if the male professional service employees can attempt to learn how to apply digital skill to do themselves jobs in order to improve efficiencies and service performance to satisfy patients, such as medical service needs, school search service needs, construction firms' building needs. Then, the owning high digital technology skillful female employees will be more easier to find the professional service jobs which need digital skill more easier than the lacking digital skill female service professionals in future global digital service professional labour market.

On the other robotic communication skill need aspect, future employers expect workers to know how to communicate with robots to work efficiently in any working environment if the employers need robotc to serve their organizations. For example, communication between the robots on factory floors, and between people and robots could allow robots to start and stopr processes based on real-time conditions around them and alert people when there is a problem, so robots could increase their own efficiency if the workers could monitor themselves and determine when they needed maintenance; efficiency would also be improved if machines and robots could make production decisions on their own by. For example, ordering new suppliers when existing inputs into a production process run low. The increase in productivity of industrial robots will likely reduce the number of manual jobs on the shop floor.

At the same time, the increased output made possible by such robots will mean that manufacturers need more people in accounting, finance, sales, advertising and other roles. The increase in putput may also drive increased employment on manufacturers' supply chains. Hence, future employers expect to employ the workers who can know how to communicate with robots to work efficiently in order to raise productivity in any working environment. It means that it the worker can know how to control and communicate with the robots to work together in the team. Then, his/ her communication and controlling robotic skill will help the organization's team to work efficiently and raise productivity in order to reduce time waste and human waste and resource waste considerately. So, future shortage of communication and controlling robotic skillful workers number will increase. It has much beneficial to workers who choose to attempt to learn how to communicate and control robots to work together in any working environment team efficiently. Because future employers will like to use robots to assist manual workers to attempt to raise productive efficiency in any working environment. So, the need of employees who know how to cooperate or communicate with robots whose talent skills will be useful to any future employers.

Future global business leaders will need human machine cooperation skill. This technological skill includes artificial intelligence (AI and internet of things (IOT), will reshape our working change. These machines will participate to our daily working environment. For instance, many business leaders agree that automated systems will free-up their time as well as they also believe they'll have more job satisfaction by offloading the tasks that they don't want to do to intelligent machines.

Therefore, future leaders will expect humans and machines can work as integrated teams within their organization in order to their workforce and machines are already successfully working this way. So, they need to expect future employees can know or learn how to work with automated systems more easily, because many jobs will be participated by automated systems, e..g simple accounting tasks, legal administration tasks etc. clerical tasks. They will be participated with (AI) technology, it learns how to cooperate with (AI) technology to finish simple clerical tasks efficiently.

Future workers will need have automated system operational skills: They include that how to operate automated systems to free -up workers' time. Workers will need to learn how to operate automated system to better with healthcare tracking devices workers will need to learn how to operate automated systems to absorb and manage information in completely different ways. Workers will need to learn how to operate automated systems of smart machines to work as admin. in any working environments. Workers need be needed to learn how to operate (AI) automated machines to make more accurate clerical tasks or efficiencies. So, the automated system (robotic) operational skillful workers‘ demand and number will increase.

In the future, employers need automated machine manufacturing and service with workers cooperation reasons include that clear protocols, will need to be established if autonomous machines fail. So, they need their workers to learn how to control and manage and communicate with autonomous machines skillfully. They believe move they depend upon technology, the more they'll have to lose in the event of a cyber attack. So, skillful workers are real required to let them to know how to cooperate with autonomous machines more efficiently and easily. Computers will need to be able to decipher between good and bad commands, so future employers have much chance to need the owning automated machines operating workers to assist any robots to make more accurate good or bad decision when robots and workers have need to make immediate judgement in their any related job responsibilities aspect.

Therefore, future owning automated machines operating workers' skillful level will be high. It bases on automated machine manufacturing environment trend factor. Finally, future technology will connect the right employee to the high task at the right time. It implies that when future global employers began to accept to apply robots to help them to raise any productivities efficiently. It will influence many manufacturing positions which need to employ any proficient skillful workers who own automated machines operational skills to know how to communicate or manage or control , even supervise any robots to work in teams in any organizational manufacturing environment efficiently.

In the future, employers also expect employees to own sufficient digital vision and strategic skills, manifest among other things. They can know how to apply data to demonstrate any senior support and sponsorship digital technological skill. They expect to reduce a skill gap and avoid a lack of employee buying and a workforce culture to change in their digital technological manufacturing organizations. Future employers also believe outdated technology that can't work fast enough, data overload, privacy and security concerns. So, it explains why it is possible that future employers also need digital working environment and automated robots machines to attempt to achieve raising productive efficient aim.

Moreover, it also explains why digital transformation need will be raised. The reasons include: They feel digital technology can gain employees' buying in , making customer experience a boardroom concern, achieving fair compensation , training and goals and strategy achievement more easily, tasking senior leaders with digital working environment change putting policies and technology to support a fully remote, flexible workforce , empowering lines of team work more efficient, teaching all employees how to code/understanding how to adopt to work with automatic machines or rots in any team efficiently. So, automate machine can raise efficiency in manufacturing society.

In conclusion, in the future business society, employees need to be stronger human machine partnerships. So , future manufacturing or service industries will have digital technology and automated machine robotic technology to assist workers to work in any working environment efficiently. They expect digital technology and automated machine robotic technology anticipation to workers' daily jobs in order to bring positive impacting to the customer experience from business owners to decision makers in marketing, customer service, research and developmnt and finance etc. They also expect technological productivity can bring positive relationship between technology and workers emerging technologies' impact on business and the way workers and automated machine work together.

In the future whether in general organizations need what kinds of employees' skills, they expect employee individual own. It is one interesting question. The common skills that employees need to own in order to any duties to any organizational departments efficiently, e.g. human resource, marketing, administrative, logistic etc. different departments. For hospital, school, business, professional occupations etc. different organizations. Whether future school ought implement one system educational method to teach different common skills to students in order to let them to leave schools to jobs more easier.

Future employers need to create new technologies including automation and algorithms, in order to create new high quality jobs and improve the job quality and productivity of the existing work of human employees in any organizations, e.g. accounting department will need intelligence (AI) to assist account clerks to do simple repeating accounting job tasks in order to share their work load and raise performance efficiency or legal organizations will need (AI) to assist law clerks to do simple repeating legal draft or legal document revising job tasks . All future general clerical jobs will apply (AI) technological tools to assist human to job, it will produce a comprehensive platform for managing workforce change.

Hence, human manual(employees) need to learn how to adopt (AI) job participation to assist them to do different kinds of simple clerical jobs in any organizational administrative departments . They , clerical employees or white color workers need to learn how manage or dominate (AI) tool to improve job performance to be better. However, (AI) administrative workforce change, it is not only one kind of job automation change role in any physical offices. It influences future administrative clerks need change a more flexible manner, utilizing remote staffing beyond physical offices and decentralization of operations organizational workforce change.

Instead of (AI) participation to administrative job aspect, (AI) will also participate to manufacturing industry environment aspect, a new human-machine manufacturing workforce change will exist to any factories, warehouses working environment. Scientists predict that in present an average of 71% of total task hours across the industries are performed by humans, compared a 29% by machines. In this average is expected to have shifted to 58% task hours performed by humans and 42% by machines. In fact, nowadays, in terms of total working hours, no work task was yet estimated to be predominantly performed by a machine or an algorithm (AI). But, this picture is predicted to have somewhat changed with machines and algorithms (AI) on average increasing their contribution to specific tasks by 57% . For example, in the future, 62% of organization's information and data processing and information search and transmission tasks will be performed by machines compared to 46% today.

Therefore, these high technological skillful job change will bring negative influence to some demotive-skillful or low skillful labors to be dismissed, if they can not upgrade or raise or re-skillful their skill level to improve their analytical thinking , technology design and programming skills to cooperate with (AI) tools to work efficiently together in any organizational manufacturing or office work environment. Because it will have many employers apply (AI) automation tools to participate with blue -color or white -color workers‘ tasks in order to raise efficiencies or improve performance in any working environment. So, it is right time to young or mid age employees need to upskill and/or reskill their rihgt type of skills to prepare future technology rich work environment changing needs.

Future technological advances will permit an increasing number of tasks traditionally performed by humans to become automated. It seems that , such automation focused primarily on routine tasks, e.g. clerical work, bookkeeping, basic paralegal work and reporting etc. However, with the advent of big data, artificial intelligence (AI), the internet of things and ever-increasing computing power , i.e. the digital revolutions, non-routine tasks are also increasingly likely to become automated. For example, the recent development in robotics and 3D printing allow firms in advanced economies to locate production closer to domestic markets in fully automated factories. As a result, the future strongest incentive to automate because of their relatively higher labour costs will be reduced, when production automated will bring the negative influence to dismiss some foolish or low productive or low skill workers , the owning high automated productive skillful workers will replace the low productive skillful workers in any factories' manufacturing environments. So, technological progress participates to raise quantity of jobs will cause result in significant job losses to low skillful workers. Because future employers will need many high automated productive employees to help them to cooperate with (AI) automated machine to work together efficiently. For example, many proportion of occupations at high risk is greatest in Germany and lowest in Korea, these countries organizations will accept to spend technology investments and education of workers to prepare future automatability manufacturing development successfully.

However, future automat ability manufacturing development will bring technological unemployment in possible, due to workers need to adjust to the challenge of automation by switching tasks. Thus, preventing technological unemployment, also technological change does not just destroy jobs, but also generates new roles through its effect on productivity and the demand for new technologies. For example, it has been estimated that, for each high tech-job created in the industries , such as computing equipment or electrical machinery, some 4.9 % additional jobs are created for lawyers, taxi, drivers and waiter in the local economy (Moretti, 2011). Therefore, automated will also influence service industries' job nature change, e.g. taxi drivers need to apply (AI) automated machines to assist them to drive their taxis. When the passenger tells the taxi driver where he/she wants to go. Then, the (AI automated machine will follow the GPS road direction map to be indicated how to drive the taxi to go to the destination automatically . So, future taxi driver is one assistance role to assist the (AI) automated driving tool to dominate the (AI) tool to drive the taxi to catch the passenger to arrive the destination safety in the short time in possible. For another example, future restaurant waiters will need (AI) automated machines's assistance to help them to deliver or dispatch any foods and soft drinks to send to the identified eater's table carefully in accurate and efficient service performance way from the kitchen, in especially in the busy time and many people are sitting in the large size restaurant environment. So, future, waiter roles will be the leader , they need to manage or control or supervise the (AI) robotics how to make decisions to arrange to dispatch which foods or soft drinks to the different tables in preference immediately. Also, future law clerks need to supervise or manage the law robotics how to help them to make decisions to do revision or draft or filing legal tasks in preference in order to avoid any typing words are mistaken to type on computers or revised draft in wrong way to assist manual legal clerks' mistaken words are appearance on any legal documents. So, the law clerk future role will be the trainer role , he/ she needs to teacher the robots how to check any words, e.g. grammars to correct them to be right grammars, or giving the accurate revision legal documents' instruction to let the legal robots to know how to revise each legal draft to prove whether which part of the legal draft will have wrong to be needed to revise.

In conclusion, future many manual workers' service or manufacturing job natures will become automated assistance to robotics. So, employees need to

upgrade their skills in order to adopt new technological work nature change.

Reference

Moretti, E. (2011) local labor market in O, Ashentelter and D. Card (eds.)

handbook of labor economics, Elsevier, North Halland.

Becoming robotic talent human how influences social changes

Nowadays we tend to think about social and digital technology more from a personal or consumer perspective than their business or professional applications, but as the Digital Era continues to progress, many of technology's most profound impacts are likely to be in the world of work. In addition to changes in product and business development, knowledge management, data analysis, and other operational processes, transforming talent management will be a key priority for organizations striving to be employers of choice.

● Digital technology encourages to create talent human

Why does digitized technology encourage to create talent human or excite human to learn new things ? The human capital implications of social and digital technologies impact virtually everyone, regardless of the type of organization they work for, their profession, their functional area, or their career stage. That means that the talent management functions in all organizations, as well as the professionals who staff and lead them, have a critical role to play in ensuring the efficient and effective transition and transformation from Industrial Era models and processes to their Digital Era upgrades.

It's no surprise that talent management has already become more "high tech." Many employment related activities have been digitized, and there has been a corresponding increase in employee self-service. It's important to remember, however, that digitization is not the same thing as digital engagement, and that the rise of "high tech" solutions doesn't necessitate the loss of a "high touch" approach to managing an organization's human assets. Transforming talent management requires digitization, to be sure, but it also involves leveraging social and digital technologies in ways that promote and enhance communication, collaboration, and engagement - not just between an employee and the organization, but between and among employees themselves.

Talent Acquisition

The logical place to start when talking about the impact of social and digital technologies on talent management is talent acquisition, where the greatest advances have been made. Anyone who has searched and applied for jobs in the past 10 years is very familiar with how technology has transformed the application process, which in most organizations (and virtually all large ones) is now almost completely digitized and automated.

However, there are other ways in which social and digital technologies are impacting talent acquisition that may not be as well-known or commonly understood. Social media sites in particular (such as Facebook, YouTube, and Pinterest) are a great way to promote an employer's brand and offer realistic previews of work life, people and culture in organizations. Online games and simulations can also be used to get a sense of what working for an organization would be like, and give organizations themselves an opportunity to determine if a prospective candidate would be a good cultural fit and potentially successful.

On organizational working environment aspect, some employers are recognizing the value of digital alumni networks or communities to maintain strong relationships with former employees. One of the primary motivations for doing this is that the employees may return one day and/or make referrals to or from their personal and professional networks. Similarly, talent networks enable organizations to establish and maintain relationships with professionals in key areas like IT and engineering, even when there isn't a current opportunity to have those folks be a part of the organization. Moreover, social media can bring positive influence to impact organizations to encourage employees to attempt or feel needs to learning new things for their tasks needs. Due to social media has actually transformed every stage of the recruiting process in significant ways - so much so that the traditional recruiting funnel can be recast in "social" terms. At the top of the funnel are activities like social advertising (i.e., placing job ads on social networks like Facebook), social sourcing (i.e., searching for candidates who meet certain criteria on networks like LinkedIn), and social referrals (i.e., having current employees share position openings with their online personal and professional networks). And at the bottom of the funnel is social screening (i.e., reviewing a candidate's public activity in social networks to identify potential hiring risks).

- Learning management is needed to feel needs to any organizations

Learning management is probably the another most advanced area when it comes to adopting and adapting to new technologies. As with recruiting and other processes, the initial advances are in the area of digitization, with social software applications evolving next. One of the obvious digital impacts is the increased use of el-earning and online learning platforms with self-paced study. There are also countless instructional videos on the web, both free and fee-based, that address a virtually unlimited range of topics. And we can't forget MOOCs - massive, open, online courses - which have proliferated in the past couple of years. Finally, many organizations have also started to leverage tablets and other mobile devices for learning, as well as using simulations and games to help employees develop specific skills. In addition to offering training through a variety of multimedia channels, organizations are increasingly using a range of digital tools for assessing employees' skills. They're also allowing employees to play an enhanced role in identifying their key skill sets and training needs, and can even have them create their own learning and development plans. Allowing employees to take a more active role in their own learning and skills management enables organizations to develop and maintain a more complete and accurate knowledge and skills database, which in turn enables them to maximize the value of the workforce in which they've already invested.

1. Formal learning management systems and platforms are also beginning to incorporate social technologies in a variety of ways. Promoting connections and interactions among participants, as well as with the instructor, can enhance the learning experience both during and after a course. Creating course-based cohorts that allow people to continue to interact with each other via a digital community - even when their shared learning experience is face-to-face - can promote both knowledge transfer and retention, in addition to increasing commitment and engagement through interpersonal connections.

2. Informal learning - which is now also referred to as social learning - is greatly enhanced by social technologies as well. In fact, this is probably the greatest opportunity and area of growth for organizations of all types and sizes. Through private social networks, intranets and other internal platforms that have incorporated social technology elements, organizations are better able to facilitate employee learning as they perform their job duties and complete work activities. Along with the networks themselves, features like advanced search, identified subject matter experts, digital communities of practice, wikis and more enable employees to access and learn from colleagues who are not just next door or down the hall, but even in another city, state or country!

As organizations move forward with leveraging technology to enhance learning initiatives, it will become increasingly important for them to address issues related to digital literacy and digital competencies. For the past several decades we've generally taken what I refer to as an LIY, or Learn It Yourself, approach to digital knowledge and skills. Although organizations may invest in teaching someone how to use a specific application related to their job, they make virtually no investment in helping individuals learn how to use general digital tools like Microsoft Office and even email. Left to their own devices, most people - and I include myself in this group- are much less efficient and effective at using these tools than they could or should be. As our tools get even more sophisticated, we need the foundational knowledge and skills to be able to use them well - and this foundation should probably be provided via more formal training. In other words, many people need to be "taught how to learn" in the Digital Era. If organizations aren't going to provide the formal training workers need to do that, it's probably in an individual's best interests to pursue those kinds of development opportunities on their own.

● What are social influences on human behavior when talent human number increases?

Social Influences on Human Behavior Because human beings are social and learn from observation rather than depending entirely on instinct, almost all aspects of human psychology and behavior are socially influenced. Languages, modes of dress, gender roles and avoided taboos are all agreed upon at a group level and form the basis of culture. What are the characteristics of social change? Small-scale and short-term changes are characteristic of human societies, because customs and norms change, new techniques and technologies are invented, environmental changes spur new adaptations, and conflicts result in redistributions of power. This universal human potential for social change has a biological basis.

This universal human potential for social change has a biological basis. It is rooted in the flexibility and adaptability of the human species—the near absence of biologically fixed action patterns (instincts) on the one hand and the enormous capacity for learning, symbolizing, and creating on the other hand. Because human beings are social and learn from observation rather than depending entirely on instinct, almost all aspects of human psychology and behaviours are socially influenced. Languages, modes of dress, gender roles and avoided taboos are all agreed upon at a group level and form the basis of culture.

On conclusion, when one country can create many talent human, e.g. students, workers. Then they can bring more positive attribution to help or assist themselves country to develop rapidly. Consequently, the country's economic growth speed will be rapid. So, I believe that it has close relationship between economy growth and talent human number to any countries in nowadays societies.

Robotics can improve internet technology development to raise economic growth factors

Why do we improve to improve internet technology? What long term social benefits will benefits if scientists can improve internet speed and research any information function ? I shall research these questions to give suggestion as below:

Why does internet improvement make life better? Internet of Things Benefits In short, the scale of change that IoT technology offers can be scary. At the same time, the benefits of a well-executed IoT strategy can be more need for an organization: Safety, Comfort, Efficiency. Also, the Internet offers teens the ability to make friends with peers with whom they would not otherwise connect. With pop culture deteriorating into many distinct subcultures, teens' interests are more variable than they have ever been. With internet communication, employees can effortlessly communicate with one another at anytime from anywhere in the world. This allows employees situated in different parts of the world to give their opinion and voice their concerns. Through internet access, individuals in developing countries are able to gain access to more of the modern economy. With internet connectivity, those living in remote areas can now easily take out microloans, participate in e-banking and more. A large share of respondents predict enormous potential for improved quality of life over the next 50 years for most individuals thanks to internet connectivity, although many said the benefits of a wired world are not likely to be evenly distributed.

- How internet can excite young to learn?

Internet can learn younger to learn much different new knowledge when they research any questions and find answers from internet channel.
As one major aspect of teen life is social environment, changes in how teens connect impact the ways in which teens develop social skills. ** Luckily, the Internet offers many social-skill enhancement opportunities for teens of all different personalities . One advantage the Internet brings that the standard school environment cannot is the ability for teens to adjust their amount of social interaction. Teens who are extremely outgoing can spend their free time in social environments both offline and online, making new connections and catching up with friends.For example, a teen who finds

large amounts of face-to-face interaction to be intimidating can use the Internet to engage in conversations while reducing the potential for social anxiety. In a way, this trains less social teens to be more social . In the past, these types of teens did not have the advantage of this social training provided by the Internet.

● Internet can encourage Social Network Growth

The Internet offers teens the ability to make friends with peers with whom they would not otherwise connect. With pop culture deteriorating into many distinct subcultures, teens' interests are more variable than they have ever been. Whereas in the past, children at school might have discussed the current top 40 when discussing music, today's kids define their musical tastes as specific genres, such as post-industrial, dubstep or jpop. Today, it's harder for teens to find peers who share the same interests in their schools. But online, not so. The Internet's social networks help teens find communities of peers who share similar interests, allowing a teen to grow his social network in a way that is specific to him 2. Today's teens are increasingly willing to make friends with different groups of people due to the ability to actually meet them, and this can be useful when they reach adulthood, a time in which accepting people of different backgrounds and demographics is crucial to career and academic growth. The Internet offers teens the ability to make friends with peers with whom they would not otherwise connect.

Today's teens are increasingly willing to make friends with different groups of people due to the ability to actually meet them, and this can be useful when they reach adulthood, a time in which accepting people of different backgrounds and demographics is crucial to career and academic growth.But the Internet can help teens foster self identity through exposure to new people, communities, hobbies and concepts. As teens go through more experiences, they learn more about themselves. And as the Internet can offer teens a wealth of experience, it can play the role of hastening the development of self identity.For many teens, the hardest part of life is figuring out identity.But the Internet can help teens foster self identity through exposure to new people, communities, hobbies and concepts.

● What Are Main Benefits of Internet Communication speed improvement ?

It may include as below:

1 Makes communication easier

Doing business through phone or mail doesn't work well ? Before the internet came into existence, the only way to communicate was through a phone. Or if you needed to send a note you had to send letters via mail. With the arrival of the Internet, staff and team managers can connect instantaneously without leaving their work place. ezTalks Meetings, a one-stop internet communication provider, is a perfect example. With this platform, participants can communicate as if they were right next to one another thanks to its quality video and audio. The tool comes with a rich set of features like screen sharing, cross platform chat, innovative whiteboard, and more.

2 Enhances collaboration

Internet communication brings teams together across the globe. Staff can collaborate easily without limitations and make more informed decisions instantaneously. This leads to reduced project timelines, cutting back on the time required to launch a new product/service. This piece of technology is also useful in education. Not only can students collaborate with foreign students, they can share ideas and learn about the diverse cultures out there. Parents can also become actively involved in their kids education by linking their children school with libraries, homes, and more. Millions of schools around the world are already using this technology to enhance learning.

3 It is cost effective

The cost of internet communication is significantly low when compared with other means of communication like face to face meetings and mail delivery. The technology connects you to your partners, colleagues, clients and suppliers from just about any location for a fraction of the cost required to host a one-on-one meeting. And as technology continues to become more efficient, the cost of online communication continues to drop significantly. With the traditional face to face meeting, you need to spare time, cash to travel and so on. Internet communication allows you and your team to connect without having to leave your offices.

4 Improves work relationships

Building a good relationship between workers spread around the globe is not easy. Business trips can negatively affect life– work balance. Team members can burn out fast if they have to make business travels that deny them the chance to participate in crucial events with friends and family. With internet communication, employees can effortlessly communicate with one another at anytime from anywhere in the world. This allows employees situated in different parts of the world to give their opinion and voice their concerns. Therefore, internet communication is an important business asset, particularly for companies that have tapped into global markets.

5 Increases productivity

While the companies of yesteryear might not have treasured effective communication, modern workplace requires both the management and the staff have the tools to effectively communicate internally and externally. This is because effective communication is important in increasing productivity as it directly impacts the behavior of the employees and how they perform. Internet communication plays an integral role in getting stuff done fast and efficiently which ultimately improves productivity. Poor communication can have a negative effect on productivity as the staff may not get the adequate info to accomplish a job they have been assigned.

6 Increases accountability

Errors slow down productivity and so it is tempting to punish or fire employees who repeatedly make errors. One major advantage of internet communication is that it helps to decrease these errors. This piece of technology pinpoints errors and how staff can avoid them. In workplaces that don't make use of various forms of internet communication, those mistakes go unnoticed. With internet communication, there is no room for mistakes as employees feel liable for their actions and safe to point out mistakes. They also feel secure expressing their ideas and suggestions in a group setting.

- Why does internet improvement can help any industries services or efficiencies improvment?

Internet improvement will revolutionize the world and lead to groundbreaking changes in transportation, industry, communication, education, energy, health care, communication, entertainment, government, warfare and even basic research. For example, self-driving cars, trains, semi-trucks, ships and airplanes will mean that goods and people can be transported farther, faster and with less energy and with massively fewer vehicles. Automated mining and manufacturing will further reduce the need for human workers to engage in rote work. Machine language translation will finally close the language barrier, while digital tutors, teachers and personal assistants with human qualities will make everything from learning new subjects to booking salon appointments faster and easier. For businesses, automated secretaries, salespeople, waiters, waitress, baristas and customer support personnel will lead to cost savings, efficiency gains and improved customer experiences. Socially, individuals will be able to find AI pets, friends and even therapists who can provide the love and emotional support that many people so desperately want. Entertainment will become far more interactive, as immersive AI experiences come to supplement traditional passive forms of media. Energy generation and health care will vastly improve with the addition of powerful AI tools that can take a systems-level view of operations and locate opportunities to gain efficiencies in design and operation. AI-driven robotics (e.g., drones) will revolutionize warfare. Finally, intelligent AI will contribute immensely to basic research and likely begin to create scientific discoveries of its own. So, it implies that internet improvement ought assist any kinds of industy service or efficiency improvement.

● Internet may become any organizational digital assets

On an individual basis, we will think about our digital assets as much as our physical ones. Ideally, we will have more transparent control over our data, and the ability to understand where it resides and exchange it for value – negotiating with the platform companies that are now in a winner-take-all position. Some children born today are named with search engine-optimization in mind; we'll be thinking more comprehensively about a set of rights and responsibilities of personal data that children are born with. Governments will have a higher level of regulation and protection of individual data. On an individual level, there will be greater integration of technology with our physical selves. For example, I can see devices that augment hearing and vision, and that enable greater access to data through our physical selves. Hard for me to picture what that looks like, but 50 years is a lot of time to figure it out. On a societal level, AI will have affected many jobs. Not only the truck drivers and the factory workers, but professions that have been largely unassailable – law, medicine – will have gone through a painful transformation. It seems entirely reasonable that a great deal of our digital lives will be focused on habitable environments: identifying them, improving them, expanding them.

Significant, often highly communication and computation technologically driven, advances in day-to-day areas like health care, safety and human services, will continue to have a significant measurable improvement in many lives, often 'invisible' as an unnoticed reduction in bad outcomes, will continue to reduce the incidence of human-scale disasters. Advances in opportunities for self-actualisation through education, community and creative work will continue. So, I believe that future many organizations may apply internet communication tool for their digital assets.

● Internet improvement may assist robotic development

Most of the focus on technology and particularly AI and machine learning developments these days is limited to virtual systems (e.g., apps for travel booking, social networks, search engines, games). I expect this to move, in the next 50 years, into networking people with machines, remotely operating in a myriad of environments, such as homes, hospitals, factories, sport arenas and so on. This will change work as we know it today, as it will change medicine (increasing remote surgery), travel (autonomous and remotely-guided cars, trains, planes), entertainment (games where real robots, instead of virtual agents, evolve in real scenarios). These are just a few ideas/scenarios. Many more, difficult to anticipate today, will appear. They will bring further challenges on privacy, security and safety, which everyone should be closely watching and monitoring. Beyond current discussions on privacy problems concerning 'virtual world' apps, we need to consider that 'real world' apps may enhance many of those problems, as they interact physically and/or in proximity with humans. So, future historians will observe that, in many ways, the rise of the internet over the next few decades will have improved the world, but it hasn't been without its costs that were sometimes severe and disruptive to entire industries and nations as well as improve robotic development.

This is similarly valid for AI.Living longer and better lives is the shining promise of the digital age. Many respondents to this canvassing agreed that internet advancement is likely to lead to better human-health outcomes, although perhaps not for everyone. As the following comments show, experts foresee new cures for chronic illnesses, rapid advancement in biotechnology and expanded access to care thanks to the development of better telehealth systems. Life will improve in multiple ways. One in particular I think worth mentioning will be improvements in health care in three distinct ways. One is significantly better medical technology related to cancer and other major diseases. The second is significantly reduced cost of health care. The third is much higher and broader availability of high-quality health care, thereby reducing the differences in outcomes between wealthy and poor citizens. So, when hospitals can improve internet communication , if the hospital can apply robots to assist doctors and nurses to serve patients. Then, internet communication can help them to cooperate more efficient.

- Internet improvement to assist 5G laptop development

Many of the technologies we see commercialized today began in government and university research labs. Fifty years ago, computers were the size of walk-in closets, and the notion of personal computers was laughable to most people. Today we're facing another shift, from personal and mobile to ambient computing. We're also seeing a huge amount of research in the areas of prosthetics, neuroscience and other technologies intended to translate brain activity into physical form. All discussion of transhumanism aside, there are very real current and future applications for technology 'implants' and prosthetics that will be able to aid mobility, memory, even intelligence, and other physical and neurological functions. And, as nearly always happens, the technology is far ahead of our understanding of the human implications. Will these technologies be available to all, or just to a privileged class? What happens to the data? Will it be 'willed' as a digital legacy to future generations? What are the ethical (and for some, religious and spiritual) implications of changing the human body with technology? In many ways, these are not new questions. We've used technology to augment the physical form since the first caveman picked up a walking stick. But the key here will be to focus as much (or more) on the way we use these technologies as we do on inventing them. All of above factors will be influenced to future 5G mobile phone by internet improvement?

Our homes, transportation, appliances, communication devices and even our clothes will be constantly communicating as part of a digital network. We have enough pieces of this today that we can somewhat imagine what it will be like. Through our clothes, doctors can monitor in real time our vital signs, metabolic condition and markers relevant to specific diseases. Parents will have real-time information about young children. The difference in the future will be the constant sharing of information, data updates and responses of all these interconnected devices. The things we create will interact with us to protect us. Our notions of privacy and even liability will be redefined. Lowering the cost and increasing the effectiveness of health care will require sharing information about how our bodies are functioning. Those who opt out may have to accept palliative hospice care over active treatment. Not keeping track of children real-time may be considered a form of child neglect. Digital will do more than connect our things to each other – it will invade our bodies. Advances in prosthetics, replacement organs and implants will turn our bodies into digital devices. This will create a host of new issues, including defining 'human' and where the line exists between that human and the digital universe – if people are always connected, always on are humans now part of the internet?

● How internet improvement influences AI provides medical service to hospitals?

Similarly, AI embedded in devices or wearables can be applied to predict and ameliorate many mental health illnesses. However, there is potential for there to be huge inequalities in our societies in the ability of individuals to access such technologies, causing both social disruption and new causes for mental health diseases, such as depression and anxiety. On balance, I am an optimist about the ability of human beings to adjust and develop new ethical norms for dealing with such issues.Surveillance technology, especially that powered by AI algorithms, is becoming more powerful and all-present than ever before. But to look at that and say that technology won't help people is absurd. Medical technology, technology to help people with disabilities, technology that will increase our comfort and abilities as humans will continue to appear and develop.The digital revolution will bring benefits in particular for health, providing personalized monitoring through Internet of Things and wearable devices. The AI will analyze those data in order to provide personalized medicine solutions.The most noticeable change for better in the next 50 years will be in health and average life expectancy. At this pace, and, taking into account the developments in digital technologies, I hope that several discoveries will reduce the risk of death, such as cancer or even death by road accident. New drugs could be developed, increasing the active work age and possibility maintaining the sustainability of countries' social health care and retirement funds. Another area AI can have impact is in creating the framework within genomics, epigenomics and metabolomics can be used to keep people healthy and to intervene when we start to deviate from health. Indeed, with AI we may be able to hack the brain and other secreting cells so that we can auto-generate lifesaving medicines, block unwanted biological processes (e.g., cancer), and coupled to understanding the brain, be able to hack at neurological disorders."

Thus, I believe that future hospitals were able to utilize internet technology to solve human health problems to make citizens' lives better and improve their access to care and services to improve their health outcomes. The benefits of the internet in the health care industry have continued to improve access to care and services, particularly for elderly, disabled or rural citizens. Digital tools will continue to be integrated into daily life to help the most vulnerable and isolated who need services, care and support. With laws supporting these groups, benefits in these areas will continue and expand to include behavioral health and resources for this group and for others. In the area of behavioral health in particular, digital tools will provide far-reaching benefits to citizens who need services but do not access them directly in person. Access to behavioral health will increase significantly in the next 50 years as a result of more enhanced and widely available digital tools made available to practitioners for delivering care to vulnerable populations, and by minimizing the stigma of accessing this type of care in person. It is a more affordable, personalized and continuous way of providing this type of care that is also more likely to attain adherence.

● The cyborg generation: Humans will partner more directly with technology when internet is popular to be used in any where

The inevitable 'Singularity' will result in changes to humans and will increase the rate of our evolution toward hybrid 'machines.' I also believe that new and modified materials will become 'smart.' For instance, new materials will be 'self-aware' and will be able to communicate problems in order to avoid failure. Ultimately, these materials will become 'self-healing' and will be able to harness raw materials to manufacture replacement parts in situ. All these materials, and the things built with them will participate in the connected world. We will see continued blurring of the line between 'real' and 'virtual' life." For exaple, artificial general intelligence and quantum computing available in a future version of the cloud connected to individual brain augmentation could make us augmented geniuses, inventing our daily lives in a self-actualization economy as the conscious-technology civilization evolves. Implants in humans that continuously connect them to the web will lead to a loss of privacy and the potential for thought control, decline in autonomy.

● Everyone agrees that the world will be putting AI to work, when internet is improvement to raise robotic efficiency and performance improvement

The technology visionaries surveyed described a much different work environment from the current one. They say remote work arrangements are likely to be the rule, rather than the exception, and virtual assistants will handle many of the mundane and unpleasant tasks currently performed by humans. The shooting is done by a drone guided by a smart guy/gal working a 9-to-5 job in an air-conditioned office in a nice town. Garbage could be picked up, sorted, recycled, all by robots with AI. Tedious surgery completed by robots and teaching via YouTube would leave the humans to the interesting and exciting cases, not the redoing of same lessons to yet more patients/students. Humans could live well on a 20-hour work week with many weeks of paid vacation. Having a job/career could become a positive, not just a necessity. With 24/7 learning and just-in-time capacity, people could change areas or careers many times with ease whenever they become bored. This positive outcome is possible if we collectively manage the creation and distribution of the tools and access to the use of new emerging tools. Thus, future everyone will have hundreds of digital workers working for them. Our cognitive mediators will know us in some ways better than we know ourselves. Better episodic memories and large numbers of digital workers will allow expanded entrepreneurship, lifelong learning and focus on transformation.

Thus, our future social development already small world will shrink further as remote collaboration becomes the norm, resulting in major social changes, among them allowing the recent concentration of expertise in major cities to relax and reducing the relevance of national borders. Furthermore, deep learning and AI-assisted technologies for software development and verification, combined with more abstract primitives for executing software in the cloud, will enable even those not trained as software engineers to precisely describe and solve complex problems. I believe the question we're facing is not 'When will machines surpass human intelligence?' but instead 'How can humans work together with machines in new ways?' Rather than worrying about an impending Singularity, I propose the concept of Multiplicity: where diverse combinations of people and machines work together to solve problems and innovate. In analogy with the 1910 High School Movement that was spurred by advances in farm automation, I propose a 'Multiplicity Movement' to evolve the way we learn to emphasize the uniquely human skills that AI and robots cannot replicate: creativity, curiosity, imagination, empathy, human communication, diversity and innovation. AI systems can provide universal access to sophisticated adaptive testing and exercises to discover the unique strengths of each student and to help each student amplify his or her strengths. AI systems could support continuous learning for students of all ages and abilities. Rather than discouraging the human workers of the world with threats of an impending Singularity, let's focus on Multiplicity where advances in AI and robots can inspire us to think deeply about the kind of work we really want to do, how we can change the way we learn and how we might embrace diversity to create myriad new partnerships. So, future AI and internet technoloy will become new partners to assist any business development, even any organizations and social development. Hence, internet improvement must be needed in order to let any businesses can apply robots to raise efficiencies and improve performance more effectively. For example, free internet-connected devices will be available to the poor in exchange for carrying around a sensor that records traffic speed, environmental quality, detailed usage logs, and video and audio recordings (depending on state law). There will be secure vote-by-internet capabilities, through credit card or passport verification, with other secure kiosks available at public facilities (police stations, libraries, fire stations and post offices, should those continue to exist in their current form). Internet and 24/7 real-time connectivity will no longer be viewed as a 'thing' independent from daily life, but integral, like electricity. This has profound psychological implications about what people assume as normal and establishes baseline expectations for access, response times and personalization of functions and information. Contrary to many concerns, as technology becomes more sophisticated, it will ultimately support the primary human drives of social connectedness and agency. As we have seen with social media, first adoption is noncritical – it is a shiny penny for exploration. Then people start making judgments about the value-add based on their own goals and technology companies adapt by designing for more value to the user . Technology is going to change whether we like it or not – expecting it to be worse for individuals means that we look for what's wrong. Expecting it to be better means we look for the strengths and what works and work toward that goal. Technology gives individuals more control – a fundamental human need and a prerequisite to participatory citizenship and collective agency. The danger is that we are so distracted by technology that we forget that digital life is an extension of the offline world and demands the same critical, moral and ethical thinking.

In future 50 years every aspect of our life will be connected, organized and hence, partly controlled, as technology platform and applications businesses will take this opportunity. A few global players will dominate the business; smaller companies (startups) will mostly have a chance in the development sector. Many institutions, such as libraries, will disappear – there might be one or two libraries that function as museums to show how it used to be. People who experienced today's world will definitely value the benefits and amenities they have through technology (human-machine/AI collaboration). If technology becomes part of every aspect of our lives we will have to give up some power and control. People thinking in today's terms will lose a certain amount of freedom, independency and control over their lives. People born after 2030 will probably just think these technologies produced changes that are mostly for the better. It has always been like this – people have always thought/said 'in the old days everything was better. The free, open internet that represented a set of decentralized connections between idiosyncratic actors will be recognized as an aberration in the history of the internet. Today's internet giants will probably be the internet giants of 50 years from now. In recent years, they've made substantial progress in curtailing innovation through acquisitions and copying. As the industry matures, they will add regulatory capture to their skill sets. For many people around the world, the internet will be a set of narrow portals where they exchange their data for a curtailed set of communication, information and consumer services. Thus, digital tools will be part of our body inside and remotely, and will assist us in decision- making constantly, so it will become second nature. Nonetheless, physical feelings will still be exclusively 'physical,' i.e., there will be a significant difference between the 'sensor-based feelings' and real body feelings, so human beings will still have some advantages over technology. This, I believe, will last forever.

CHAPTER FIVE

Limiting robotic invention brings economic growth

employment ratio growth, job creating growth, unemployment ratio reduces, consumption growth, productive industries growth, service provision and service needs increases. So, it seems that any countries‘ social development , when it can have positive impact growth for any one of these issue. It implies that the country's economic is growing.

To discuss AI and economic growth issue, it may being these two main questions. Whether robotic invention may have direct or indirect relationship to influence any countries' economic growth? What are the main factors to cause robotics invention to bring the country's economic growth in its society?

On the first hand, some researchers believe that robotic invention may influence any countries‘ economic growth. However, otherwise, other many researchers find large and robust negative effects robots on employment and wages. They estimate what are more robot per thousand workers reduces the employment -to-population rate by between 0.18 and 0.34 percentage points, and is associated with a wage decline of between 0.25 and 0.5 percentage. Because many jobs can be replaced by robotics. So, it seems that robotics invention can reduce workers number and increasing wage level, even robotic increasing number, it can influence unemployment ratio increases to the country. But, some lecturers estimate that it can impact economic growth. They estimate that AI may deliver an additional economic output of around US$13 trillion by 2030 year, increasing global GDP by about 1.2% annually. This will mainly come from substitution of labour by automation and increased innovation in products and services.

What is the impact of robots on society? They may include this spillover, one robot per thousand workers has slightly less of an impact on the population as a whole, leading to an overall 0.2% point reduction in the employment-to-population ratio, and reducing wages by 0.42%. Thus, adding one robot reduces employment nationwide by 3.3 workers. So, it seems that robotic number increases may influence global workers number increases many influence global workers number reduces as the same time. It can cause unemployment workers number increases in societies.

On the other side, robotic invention can increase productivity, because robots increase productivity, which means that fewer human hours are needed to produce a given output. But, higher productivity also reduces production costs and output prices. Consequently, robotic production anticipation , it can increase the quality demanded by consumers, and firms hire workers in this increased demand.

But, when robotic production participation to any industrial manufacture, it can also bring negating effects, when they are entering the workforce, e.g. higher maintenance and installation costs to factories, enhanced risk of data breach and other cybersecurity issues, reduced flexibility, anxiety and insecurity regarding the future social development. So, it seems that robotic invention can bring the future of workplace automation may reduce workers number of factories, loss of jobs and reduced employment opportunities to global future workers, potential job lose, initial investment costs to employers. However, AI may also bring harmful to our future societies because if AI surpasses humanity in general intelligence and becomes " superintelligent" , then it could become difficult or impossible for humans to control. Moreover, a second source concern is that a sudden and unexpected " intelligence explosion" might take an unprepared human race by surprise. Hence, robotic invention may become human enemy or soldier, if human applies it to social damage aspect.

However, robotic invention can also bring advantages to our future societies in possible, robotic automation may bring advantages to employers : cost effectiveness, improved quality assurance, increased productivity, avoiding workers need to work in hazardous environments. But,. AI can also bring positive impact our daily lives, such as artificial intelligence can dramatically improve the efficiencies of our workplace and can argument the work humans can do. When AI takes over repetitive or dangerous tasks, it frees up the human workforce to do work, they are better equipped for, tasks that involve creativity and empathy among others.

However, robotic invention may bring organizational benefits in our societies. Robots will have a profound effect on the workplace of the future.

They will become capable of taking on multiple roles in organizations, e.g bookkeeping or writing law draft simple clerical tasks. So, it's time for us to start thinking about the way we shall interact with our new coworkers. To be more precise, robots are expected to take over half of all low-skilled jobs in our societies, e.g. cleaning , warehouse picking up delivering tasks, restaurant cooking, hotel front line customer service, hotel room food delivery tasks etc.

So, when robots would be used in many fields all over the world. However, robots can not totally rule over the workplace by replacing all humans at jobs to keep economy afloat. Hence, robots in the workplace may bring advantages, they will not have bad emotion problems, such as safety of utilizing robotics to work in dangerous workplace. Robots do not get distracted or need to take breaks robots never need to sleep or they need to divide their attention between a multitude of things, perfection, let employees to feel happier and safe to work when robotics can help workers to work in dangerous warehouses or factories, workers can be replaced from robotics, increases productivities and job creation , even raises efficiencies in any workplaces.

In our future, whether robots won't destroy humans. It depends on how humans choose to apply this technological worker tool. A robot may not injure a human being or, though inaction, allow a human bring to come to harm. A robot must obey the orders given it by human beings, expect where such orders would conflict with the first law. A robot must protect its existence as long as such protection does not conflict with the first or second laws. How AI technology affects us in the future. They are concerned that we will see increases in stress, anxiety, and depression as digital lives expand. Meanwhile , we shall need to adapt our future digital living, there will be less face-to-face interaction , increased inactivity, poor in-person communication skills and an overall distrust among people. For robotic invention case example, future robotics can may focus on developing these five major field: Human -robotic interface, mobility, manipulation, programming, sensors and their importance to robotics development.

Robots can be applied to educational aspect. Robots can be used to bring students into the classroom that otherwise might not be able to attend. Robots such as the one mentioned are able to bring school to student who can not present physically. Simulators-high school sees the strongest example of stimulators within drivers' education courses, e.g. Google's worker robots. Google is planning to produce worker robots with personalities. So, robots can help teachers automate key classroom processes, integrate advanced technologies, acclimate students to technological change and helping identify personalized learning potential and discovering key learning trends.

● How manufacturers to raise efficiency in order to improve economic growth

(AI) can be defined as the capability of a machine to imitate intelligent human behavior. If AI can imitate any talent humans to learn how to improve their behaviors, e.g. manufacturing industry worker behavior improves to raise GDP growth or productive number grows rapidly . Can artificial intelligence being labour to become automated? Allows an ever-in-to increasing number of tasks previously performed by human labour to become automated in the ordinary production of goods and services process.

Can (AI) create new ideas and technologies to help businessmen to solve complex problems and improve automation in the production of goods and services. The question concerns how (AI) manufacturing technology can impact economic growth?

(AI)'s new form of automation live, self-driving cars, or they may bring high levels of skill,such as legal services, radiology, and some forms of scientific lab-based research. Can it allow our societies be impacted on economic growth, due to automation to disicipline our modeling of AI.

In fact, AI automation to production of new ideas to future any industrial manufacturing process. It can influence to market structure, organization restructure, reallocation and wage inequality. So, discovering to AI automation can help future any organizations need to change existing task or discovering new tasks that can be used in production a reflects the fraction of tasks that have been automated.

It brings automating old tasks when automated could be constant, leading a stable , capital share and a stable growth rate. Hence, in long term, AI automation manufacturing technology may help businessmen to reduce large manufacturing cost in order to achieve stable micro economic benefit to them when they can apply AI automation manufacturing technologies to improve their productivities in efficient manufacturing method. For Coca Cora soft drink example, if Coca Cora applies AI automation to raise its productive soft drinks number. Then , it can manufacture many soft drinks number in short time per day. Then, its sale number can be increased, when it has enough number to supply to global to sell its soft drink. Consequently, soft drink sale number must grow rapidly significantly.

The fact that automated goods are produced with cheap capital , but it can also help business to raise production number significantly . How this superintelligence affect the economy? It seems physical tasks are essential to producing output, but when the manufacturer applies robotics to help production . Then, employees number may reduce, due to robotic participation, wages expenditure may reduce , but production number may increase .

So, AI increases the motivation at physical tasks. Hence, AI must may bring production growth innovation incentives to any manufacturers. Finally, with imitation and learning being performed mainly by super machine in developed economies. Then , research labor would become devoted to product innovations increasing product variety or inventing new products (new product lines), to replace existing products.

It is one good example to explain that how AI can bring long term social economic benefit to any manufacturers, when any old (existing) product lines are improved to innovative new product line by robotic manufacturing participation. Moreover, AI can change market structure to be reduced competition. When be escape competition effect tends to dominate at low discouragement effect may dominate for higher levels of competition or in less advanced economies. Hence , AI can also affect innovation and growth through potential effects, it might have on product market competition. So, it seems that (AI) can respond on helping social economic growth principle.

On conclusion, although robotic invention may bring disadvantages to raise unemployment ratio in possible when there are many low-skilled jobs are replaced by robotics, but at the same time, robotic may be applied to education aspect, when we are experiencing digital knowledge social development stage. Hence, smart robots ought may help humans to raise economic long term growth in possible when robotics can help the developing countries to develop more rapid to be developed countries as well as they can help the developed countries to develop more advanced both in global whole one economic developed societies. So, when robots can assist any countries to cooperate together, any countries are not independent, we need robots to assist develop between countries. Then, robots can assist any countries to develop economic growth in possible in future this day comes.

How robotic helps to solve recession
Is the use of robots to job market increasing during the Great Recession? Some researchers constructed a measure of the use of robots—commonly referred to as "robot intensity"—to estimate trends in robot exposure across more than 250 metropolitan areas and over time, finding that: During the Great Recession, robot intensity plummeted. But since 2009, robot intensity has sharply increased nationwide. They felt that robots may influence recession in possible. How are robots going to affect our jobs? Most analysis tends to be prospective in nature, and estimates of future impacts on employment vary widely, with some studies predicting that as many as 50 percent of all workers are at risk of losing their jobs to automation. Even less is understood about the actual impacts of robots on jobs, wages, and workers today. If there are many low skillful jobs e.g. cleaner, warehouse deliver, cooker, restaurant waitor etc., even high skillful jobs, e.g. accountant, lawyer, doctors etc. occupations are replaced by robotics. Then, our societies will increase unemployed people number. Consequently, great recession will be caused by robotic workers because when our societies have many people lose jobs, then many people loss income, then our consumption desires may be influenced to reduce. Consequently, many businesses may lose many customers. Low consumption desires may bring serious recession to any countries, due to robotic workers number increases to replace human workers in global societies.

The reason is that new technologies of the period have enabled people to be very productive while working part-time. Businesses do not need large numbers of employees, so individuals can devote most of their waking hours to hobbies, volunteering, and community service. In conjunction with periodic work stints, they have time to pursue new skills and personal identities that are independent of their jobs. Developed countries may be on the verge of a similar transition. Robotics and machine learning have improved productivity and enhanced the economies of many nations. Artificial intelligence (AI) has advanced into finance, transportation, defense, and energy management. The internet of things (IoT) is facilitated by high-speed networks and remote sensors to connect people and businesses. In all of this, there is a possibility of a new robotic society that could improve the lives of many people, but it also encourage future businesses apply robotics to replace human workers to do many jobs in finance, transportation, defense and energy management, medical health, hotel, tourism, cinema, theatre etc. entertainment service fields. So, robotics may bring reducing cost benefits to businessmen, but they can also increase workers losing jobs number in our societies if future many businesses make decision to apply robotics to replace human workers to do any simple ot complex jobs in global job market.

A McKinsey Global Institute analysis of 750 jobs concluded that "45% of paid activities could be automated using 'currently demonstrated technologies' and . . . 60% of occupations could have 30% or more of their processes automated."[6] A more recent McKinsey report, "Jobs Lost, Jobs Gained," found that 30 percent of "work activities" could be automated by 2030 and up to 375 million workers worldwide could be affected by emerging technologies.

Researchers at the Organization for Economic Cooperation and Development (OECD) focused on "tasks" as opposed to "jobs" and found fewer job losses. Using task-related data from 32 OECD countries, they estimated that 14 percent of jobs are highly automatable and another 32 have a significant risk of automation. Although their job loss estimates are below those of other experts, they concluded that "low qualified workers are likely to bear the brunt of the adjustment costs as the automatibility of their jobs is higher compared to highly qualified workers."

reference

James Manyika, Susan Lund, Michael Chui, Macques Bughin, Jonathan Woetzel, Parul Batra, Ryan Ko, and Saurabh Sanghui, "Jobs Lost, Jobs Gained: Workforce Transitions in a Time of Automation," McKinsey Global Institute, December, 2017.

Melanie Arntz, Terry Gregory, and Ulrich Zierahn, "The Risk of Automation for Jobs in OECD Countries," Organization for Economic Cooperation and Development, Working Paper 189, 2016.

However, some economists felt opposite opinions, they believes that future many businesses won't choose whole applying robotics to replace human workers in global job market. So, they are only human workers assistant role. Economists have, on the whole, been fairly discuss about the impact of robots and AI on workers. History is strewn with incorrect predictions of the looming irrelevance of human labour. The economic statistics have yet to signal the arrival of a robot-powered job apocalypse. Outside of slumps, firms remain keen to hire humans, for example. Growth in productivity—which ought to be surging if machines are helping fewer workers produce more output—has been unimpressive. A look beneath the aggregate numbers, though, reveals that change is indeed afoot. They believes that an AI-induced change in the mix of jobs need not translate into less hiring overall. If new technologies largely assist current workers or boost productivity by enough to spark expansion, then more AI might well go hand-in-hand with more employment. This does not appear to be happening. Instead the authors find that firms with more AI-vulnerable jobs have done much less hiring on net; that was especially the case in 2014-18, when AI-related vacancies in the database surged. But the relationship between greater use of AI and reduced hiring that is present at the firm level does not show up in aggregate data, the authors note. Machines are not yet depressing labour demand across the economy as a whole. As machines become cleverer, however, that could change.

Take work by Daron Acemoglu and David Autor of the Massachusetts Institute of Technology, Jonathon Hazell of Princeton University and Pascual Restrepo of Boston University, which was presented at the recent meeting of the American Economic Association (AEA). The authors use rich data provided by Burning Glass Technologies, a software company that maintains and analyses fine-grained job information gleaned from 40,000 firms. They identify tasks and jobs in the dataset that could be done by AI today (and are therefore vulnerable to displacement). Unsurprisingly, the researchers find that businesses that are well-suited to the adoption of AI are indeed hiring people with AI expertise. Since 2010 there has been substantial growth in the number of AI-related job vacancies advertised by firms with lots of AI-vulnerable jobs. At the same time, there has been a sharp decline in these firms' demand for capabilities that compete with those of existing AI.

An AI-induced change in the mix of jobs need not translate into less hiring overall. If new technologies largely assist current workers or boost productivity by enough to spark expansion, then more AI might well go hand-in-hand with more employment. This does not appear to be happening. Instead the authors find that firms with more AI-vulnerable jobs have done much less hiring on net; that was especially the case in 2014-18, when AI-related vacancies in the database surged. But the relationship between greater use of AI and reduced hiring that is present at the firm level does not show up in aggregate data, the authors note. Machines are not yet depressing labour demand across the economy as a whole. As machines become cleverer, however, that could change.

Evidence that AI affects labour markets primarily by taking over human tasks is at odds with some earlier studies of how firms use the technology.

A paper from 2019 by Timothy Bresnahan of Stanford University argues that the most valuable applications of AI have nothing to do with displacing humans. Rather, they are examples of "capital deepening", or the accumulation of more and better capital per worker, in very specific contexts, such as the matching algorithms used by Amazon and Google to offer better product recommendations and ads to users. To the extent that AI leads to disruption, it is at a "system level", says Mr Bresnahan—as Amazon's sales displace those of other firms, say.

New work by Ajay Agrawal, Joshua Gans and Avi Goldfarb of the University of Toronto suggests that this state of affairs may not persist for long, though. As the quality of AI predictions improves, they write, it becomes increasingly attractive for AI-using firms to restructure in more radical ways. At some level of accuracy, for example, Amazon's ability to predict consumers' desires could encourage the firm to adjust its business model—by pre-emptively shipping goods to consumers before they ever go searching at Amazon in the first place—in ways that are likely to change how many workers and of what sort the firm requires. In that event, the influence of AI on the economy could change dramatically. So, such as Amazon case, it applies robotics are only concentrated on predicting consumer prediction aspect, AI is only assistant role to Amazon human market researchers. They help Amazon market researchers to gather consumer behavior data , but Amazon human market researchers need to do marketing analysis tasks by themselves. So, Amazon can not employ human market reseachers jobs position in itself company. Amazon needs robotic and human market researchers to do market research tasks in order to achieve how to predict consumer behavior more accurately. Thus, it seems that future large enterprises won't fire any professional staffs more easily because some complex tasks, e.g. analysis tasks, they believe that human's analysis can make more accurate judgement to compare AI's analysis.

However, some scientists believe that some skilful professional occupations , they have possible be replaced by robotic. Will Architects and Engineers be Replaced by Robots? It's not uncommon for people to think they may be replaced by a robot in the workplace. After all, it's happened plenty of times before. For example, the rise of the mechanical assembly line saw machines replace people in the early 20th century. With recent advances in artificial intelligence (A.I.), it's entirely possible that more jobs are at risk. Even skilled workers, such as architects, programmers and engineers may be at risk. One day, an A.I. software developer may be able to do everything that a human programmer can do.

Recent reports have not abated this thought process. In fact, the 2016 Economic Report of the President seemed to suggest that artificial intelligence is playing an increasingly important role in the engineering industry. Just think about the software you use in your work. Many software packages can handle a lot of the complex calculations for you. Yes, this cuts down on the amount of work you do. However, this automation may also present a threat to your job. What if the future sees these same software packages handling data input, as well as processing.

Automation is important. The use of artificial intelligence, alongside various other technologies, has always improved production. More work gets done, which means that businesses make more money. Architects and engineers constantly look for ways to speed up their work. The desire for automation has informed many recent software innovations. Furthermore, project methodologies, like Building Information Modelling, place automation at the fore. That's great for speed and efficiency, but what does it mean for architects and engineers? History has shown that automation has a very human effect. People lose their jobs because machines can do them faster. Just think of it from a business viewpoint. Do you want to pay 10 or more employees, or invest in one machine? More often than not, the machine will cost less than the employees, even if you factor maintenance into the equation. It's a simplification, but not an invalid one. Businesses make these sorts of decisions all the time. By pushing for automation, architects and engineers may be slowly working themselves out of their own jobs.

Several studies have also suggested that artificial intelligence may cause job losses. One recent example comes from the University of Oxford. The study found that over 700 types of jobs are at risk of technological disruption. All told, this means that about 47% percent of jobs are at risk because of artificial intelligence. That is a huge amount of people who may find themselves obsolete due to advancing technology. The same study also mentioned a concept called the "technological bottleneck". The researchers used this to determine how "at risk" a job was of displacement. The bottleneck takes three factors into account:

•How much creative intelligence the role needs

•If manual manipulation and perception is required

•The role of social intelligence in the role

If a role requires a high degree of any of those three things, it's less likely that it's at risk from artificial intelligence. Architects and engineers are a good example. These professionals require a great deal of creative intelligence. Artificial intelligence and robots may not be able to emulate that creative intelligence. As a result, it's unlikely that architects and engineers need to worry about losing their jobs. Right now, at least. The study concluded with a cautionary note. It said that just because automation enhances an architect and engineer's work right now, it doesn't mean that automation won't replace that role in the future. So, if future human architects or engineers jobs can be replaced to do by robotics. Then, robotic architects can help the architectural firms to design more attractive architectural plans to satisfy construction firms clients needs in short time or robotic engineers can help the engineering design firms to design more attractive machines to satisfy any engineeing customers needs in short time , when robotics can be invented to own excellent creative ability to compare human architects or engineers. So, these two professional occupations will be lost when robotic architects and robotic engineers can be invented to own excellent creative ability to compare human architects or engineer in future one day in possible.

However, robotic architects or engineers may bring advantages and disadvantages both aspects:

On advantages aspect:

Artificial intelligence allows us to do all of the following:

•The completion of mundane tasks that would otherwise take a lot of labour hours. Automating such tasks frees up skilled workers to work on more important tasks.

•A.I. is not as prone to making errors as a person. As long as the A.I.'s programming is good enough, you should find that calculating errors and similar issues become problems of the past.

•Speed is a key feature of artificial intelligence. Huge datasets no longer provide any problems to businesses, as automation allows for much faster processing. This means that a business can spend money elsewhere.

•The most complex A.I.s reduce the amount of risk attached to the decision-making process. The "Curiosity" Mars rover is a good example. It's programmed to choose the best course of action depending on its position.

On disadvantages aspect:

It's not all good, unfortunately. The following are some of the bad points of artificial intelligence:

•The previously mentioned job losses can cause all sorts of problems for staff morale.

•Some believe that artificial intelligence gets rid of the human element. The nightmare scenarios in films like "The Terminator" may seem far-flung, but that doesn't mean there isn't a risk in letting machines make all the decisions.

•A.I. relies on pre-existing knowledge, which means it lacks creativity. Attempting to use it for creative endeavours may result in failure.

•Algorithms may not be able to make judgement calls in disaster situations. Again, the A.I. may not take the human element into account, no matter what's actually happening on the ground.

Oe people management aspect, what do you think would be the reaction to a robot attempting to manage people? It's likely that a lot of people won't take to kindly to artificial intelligence telling them what to do. Many underestimate the importance of people skills in the architecture and engineering profession. Architects and engineers must be able to organise workloads and manage individuals. It is sure, A.I. device could handle the former. Scheduling is a task that many already automate. However, A.I. will fall down when it comes to the human relationships that are so vital in a team environment. An A.I. won't understand when somebody is demotivated, or why. It won't make allowances for the human issues that affect every problem. This makes skilled team members even more valuable. As A.I. takes an increasing role in the workplace, the need for people management will become more important. Architects and engineers with those skills may even find they make more money to employ them. Although, it is possible that AI can replace human architects or engineers to do their tasks to be better , it can help any one architectural or enginering firms to improve design performace in order to satisfy customers design demand, but our societies will increase unemployment ratio to engineers and architects number, even universities will reduce architect and engineering students number. Our traditional professional knowledge will be felt to be rubblish when these professional subjects won't be useful to help us to find jobs easily. So, AI invention will influence many students won't choose to study these two subjects. Our societies will be influence to experience knowledge recession when knowledge will become rubblish because robotics invention , it can do many human professional jobs to do. " knowledge recession" will be important factor to bring economic recession, because human can not be encouraged to learn any new knowledge to prepare to enter job market due to robotic invention can replace us to do more complex tasks in our future societies.

Can robotic leadership be good solution method when recession had come to the country?

On leadership management aspect, can robots become clever leadership to any organizations? As artificial intelligence becomes further embedded into our everyday working lives, we are already seeing the footprint of machine learning, automation, algorithms and robots in many of our professions and sectors. However, when we look at the upper levels of business management and leadership, these technological shifts are less evident, with C level Executives continuing to lead and strategise as they have done before. In Ireland, there are more than 500 CEOs. The question is, when will we start to see machines and robots play a more central role in the CEO sphere, and is a 'Robot CEO' realistic in the short to medium term?

New research shows that 24% of people aged 25-29 would replace their boss with a robot, demonstrating an interesting trend among Generation Z. However, these data sets are perhaps less founded in AI and robotics and more in current employee engagement. It's telling that the 20-30% of people who would willingly replace their human boss with a robot is about the same percentage of people who are consistently classified as "actively disengaged" at work. In addition, research from analytics giant Gallup demonstrates that 70% of how we feel about work, namely our emotional commitment, is driven by who our manager is, again underlining the centrality of human behavioural traits when making decisions on leadership.

As the Irish economy moves forward, values will define how we use and leverage the potential of AI. Tomo Noda of the Harvard Business Review believes that we will need more focus on leadership with humanity, ethics and integrity, stating "only good people can create good AI."With many roadblocks and challenges for the economy looming, primarily in the shape of Brexit and trade tariffs, it is a sound integration of both human and tech which will provide the leadership required to ensure our economy remains robust. Human leaders have played a central role in helping to steer us out of the 2008 recession, and with diplomacy and relationship building key to our post-Brexit future, humans will undoubtedly be the key influencers within the C level for decades to come. Hence, it seems that future organizations ought choose to apply robots to assist leaders to do make important decision, if robotics can assist leaders to make any important decision to conclude the best results to improve any companies performance. Then, GDP may be influenced to increase or grow rapidly, when recession had come to the country. So, robotic leadership may be one solution to solve recession method in possible.

The Recession Cometh and Robots are Ready

In economic demand vs. supply theory indicates that consumer appetites for customized product and their expectations for ever-lowering costs. So the current tug-of-war over if, when, and where a recession will hit is not unchartered territory. For manufacturers, though, the uncertainty is particularly challenging, as the flexibility that allows operations to reflect the pace of the economy simply isn't there. The economy has been growing. Unemployment is down. Last year's Christmas sales were better than they've been in a long time. All good and logical reasons for manufacturers to hire.

Recently though, there have been signs that instability is coming. The US stock market experienced extreme volatility as 2018 came to a close. The Federal Reserve raised interest rates and laid down some pretty clear language that more was to come. Consumer confidence fell. In the UK, a deal on Brexit that would allow British manufacturers to continue to do business with the EU seemed elusive at best. The Chinese government announced that growth in its economy has slowed. And the "R" word started to appear with more frequency. These are not signs that inspire confidence. So, manufacturers once again find themselves in a place they know so well. The rock: the need to hire workers to keep ahead of demand. Compounding this challenge is that unemployment is low and it is very hard to find people with the skills needed to take a job in manufacturing and be ready to work on day one. The hard place: overwhelmingly, today's automation is fixed, expensive, and able to perform only a single task.

As one supply chain executive of a global automotive firm shared recently, "In a downturn...it is about flexibility. All of the automation we have cost too much and it is too complicated to change what it does. What we need is flexible automation that can respond when and how we need it to."Can robotics be applied to manufacturing industry to avoid cost reduces to manufacturers when consumption number reduces or recession is coming? So what makes the most sense? Hire, hoping that if and when recession comes, it will be short-lived and you won't have to lay folks off? Or try to invest in reconfiguring existing automation?

Hence, cobots give manufacturers the flexibility they need to thrive in good times and not-so-good times. Advances in robotic technology make it

possible to put cobots to work
•at lower costs
•on more than a single task
•in the same amount of time, it takes to train a person – or even less

On conclusion, with collaborative robots, manufacturers can build the operations they need to compete and thrive regardless of the economic climate, where manufacturing robotic participation can help organizations to reduce labours number on strategic tasks and flexibility is part of the organizational human resource cost reducing strategy. It seems that robotic manufacturing workers can help organizations to reduce manufacturing cost when recession is coming. Consequently, these applying manufacturing robotic businesses may prolong business life time in possible. So, it seems that manufacturing robots may help organizations to reduce manufacturing cost to keep life when recession is coming. Robots are applied to manufacture industry, manufacturing robots ought bring global economic development.

Reference

Adrian, P. (2012). Introduction to marketing theory & practice, 3 rd edition, London: Oxford press.

Ajzen, I (1991). The theory of planned behavior. Organizational behavior and human decision processes, 50(2), 179-211. doi: 10.1016/0749.5978 (91) 90020-7.

Alba, Joseph W. and J. Wesley Hutchinson (1987). " Dimensions Of Consumer Expertise", Journal of consumer research, 13 March, 411-454.

Bailey, L., Mokhtarian, P.L. Little, A. (2008). The broader Connection Between Public Transportation, Energy Conservation And Greenhouse Gas Reduction, Report Prepared As Part Of TCRP Project J-11/Tasks Transit Cooperative Research Program, Transportation Research Board Submitted To American Public Transportation Association in http://www.apta.com/research/into/online/land_use.cfmi, accessed 17 April 2008.

Baucer, R,"Consumer Bhavior As Risk Taking , In Risk Taking And Information handling In Consumer Behavior", D. Coxceds Harvard University Press, Cambridge, Mass 1976.

Biederman, P. (2008). Travel and tourism, Pearson Prentice Hall, New Jersey.

Bogers, R. P., Brug, J. Van Assema, P., & Dagnetie, P.C. (2004) , Explaining fruit and vegetable consumption: The theory of planned behavior and misconception of personal intake level. Appetite, 42,157-166.

Bolton, Ruth N. (1998), " A Dynamic Model Of The Duration Of The Customer's Relationship With A Continuous Service Provider: The Role Of Satisfaction", Marketing Science, 17 (1), 45-65.

B.Shiv and A. Fedorikhin, " Heart And Min In Conflict: The Interplay Of affect And Cognition In Consumer Decision Making", J. Consumer Res., vol. 26, pp. 278-292, Dcc. 1999.

Brown, K.W., Ryan, R.M. Reswell , J.D. (2007). Mindfulness: Theoretical Foundatins And Evidence For Its Salutary Effects. Psychological Inquiry, 18, 211-237.

Burke, R.R. : Behavioral effects of digital signage, J. Advertising Res. 49(2), 180-185 (2009).

Cant, M., Brink , A. & Brijall, S., Consumer behavior, Cape Town, South Africa: Juta, 2006.

Conner, M. & Abraham, C. (2001). Conscientiousness and the theory of planned behavior: Toward a more complete model of the antecedents of intention and behavior. Social psychology bulletin, 27, 1547-1561.

Cooper C. Mallon, K, Leadbetter S, Pollack L, Peipins (2005) , cancer internet search activity on a major search engine, United States 2001 to 2003, J Med Internet Res. 7(3): e36.

Cope, R. R. Cope and H. Davis (2008). Disney's virtual Queues: A strategic opportunity to co-brand services ? Journal of Business & economics research, vol. 6 no10, 13-20.

Cornelia, B.F. (1999) Rural development news, the North Central Regional Center For Rural Development vol. no 24 , IOWA.

Couper, M.P. J. Blair and T. Triplet (1999). A Comparison Of Mail And E-mail For a Survey Of Employees In USA Statistical Agencies. Journal Of Official Statistics, 15, 39-56.

David J. Nowak & Gordon M. Melsler (2016) " Air quality effects of urban trees and parks." National recreation and park association, USA.

Data monitor (2008). The proctor and gamble company. Retrieved Nov. 15 2009 from http://www.datamonitor.com/

De Hollander, A. E. M., J.M. Melse, Elebret & P. G.N. Kramers (1999), " An Aggregate public health indicator to represent the impact of multiple environmental exposures" Epidemiology: 606-617.

De Visser, R.O., & McDonnell, E.J. (2013). " Man points": Masculine capital and young men's health. Health psychology, 32(1), 5-14. doi:10. 1037/a0029045.

Dunn, J & A Neumsister (2002). Knowledge management in the Information age. E. business review, Fall , 37-45. Jounral of service, spring 2011, vol. 4, no1, De Grovte (2009).

Dyer, D., F. Dalzell & R. Olegario (2004). Rising tide. Lessons learned from 165 years of brand building at Procter and Gamble. Boston, MA: Havard Business School Press.

Eysenbach G (2006) Infodemiology: Tracking flu- related searches on the web for syndromic surveillance. American Medical Informatics Associaion Annual Symposium Proceedings , Curran Associates, Red Hook,

NY, pp. 244-248.

Ettredge M, Gerdes, J. Karuga , G (2005) Using web- based search data to predict macro-economic statistics. Commun ACM 48: 87-92.

Felce, D. and Perry, J. (1995). Quality of life: A contribution to its definition and measurement, vol. 16, no.1 pp: 51-74.

Feldman, Jack M. And John G. Lynch Jr. (1988), "Self-Generated Validity And Other Effects Of Measurement On Belife, Attitude, Intention And Behavior", Journal of applied psychology, 73(3),421-35.

Fiese, M, Hofmann, W., & Wanke, M (2009). The impulsive consumer. Predicting consumer behavior with implicit reaction time measurement. In M. Wanke (ed.) Social psychology of consumer behavior (pp.335-364). New York, NY: Psychology press.

Fitzsimons, Gavan, J. And Vicki G. Morwitz (1996), " The Effect Of Measuring Intent On Brand-Level Purchase Behavior", Journal of consumer research, 23 (1), 1-11.

Hallerman , D. (2008) video Advertising Online: Spending And Pricing , New York. E-Marketer.

Harriet Griffey. (2010) The art of concentration, enhance focus, Reduce, stress and achieve move. Macmillan publishers ltd,Basinastoke and Oxford, London UK.

Helleman, D. (2008) Video Advertising Online: Spending And Pricing , New Y ork, E-Marketer.

Hensen, C. (2003). Kreuzfahrtourismus.www.christoph- hensen.de/ Facharbeit.pdf.

Huang, H.I. (2012). An empirical analysis of the strategic Management of competitive advantage: a case study of higher technical and vocational education in Taiwan (Doctoral dissertation, Victoria University).

Jamieson, Linda F. And Frank M. Bass (1989), " Adjusting Stated Intention Measures To Predict Trial Purchase Of New Products: A Comparison Of Models And Methods," Journal of marketing research, 26 (August), 336-45.

Korea Ministry Of Environment. Public Organizations spend 2.2 Trillon Korean Won To Purchase green Products in 2014; Ministry Of Environment: Sejoung, Korea, 2015.

Kremers, S.P. J., De Bruijn, G.J., droomers, M., Van Lenthe, F. J., & Brug, J. (2005). Environmental interventions for selected dietary behaviors in adults. In J. Brug & F. J. Van Lenthe (eds.) , Environmental determinants and interventions for physical activity, nutrition and smoking: A review pp. 282-315. Rotterdam: Erasmus Medical Center.

Lee, D.; Kim, M. ; Lee, J. adoption of green electricity policies: Investigating the role of environmental attitudes via big data-driven search-queries. Energy policy 2016. 90, 187-201.

Lee, Terrence, " Tech in Asia-connecting Asia's startup system " Tech. in Asia- connecting Asia's startup ecosystem, N.p.,4 July 2016.

Los Angeles Country Department Of public Health (2016), Country Health Ranking Model, Retrieved From www.countryhealthrankgings.org/our-approach. USA.

Mayne, Lonnie. " Evolve of die in the age of the consumer". Entrepreneur, N.P. , 16 Apr. 2014. web of Oct. 2016.

McGregor, S.L. T., & Goldsmith, E.B. (1998). Expanding our understanding of quality of life, standard of living and well-being. Journal of family and consumer science, 90(2), 2-6, 22.

McMichael, A.J. M. Mckee, J. Shkolnikov and T. Valkanen (2004), " Morality trends and setbacks, global convergence or divergence?", Lancet 363, 1155-1159.

Melse, J.M. & A.E. M. De Hollander (2001). " Human Health And The Environment", background document for the OECD Environmental Outlook, OECD, Paris.

Moschis, George p. & Roy, L. Moore (1979), " Decision making among the young. A socialization perspective " Journal of consumer research , 6 (September).

Mulligan, M. Banerjee, T & Thomas, N. (2008) ,European Paid Content And Activity Forecast, (2008 to 2013), Jupiter Research.

Peter, J., Ryan, M, M, " An Investigation Of Perceived Risk At The Brand Level, " Journal of marketing research, 13 May 1976, pp. 184-188.

Pieters, R., & Wedel, M. (2007). Goal Control Of Visual Attention To Advertising: The Yarbus Implication. Journal Of Consumer Research, 34, 224-233 (August).

Parasuaman, and Leonard L. Berry (1985), " Problems And Strategies In Sevices Marketing", Journal of marketing, 49 (Spring), 33-46.

Priesnitz, W. (2007) Counting Our Food Miles. Natural Life, 1 July.

R.C. Oliver, " When is consumer loyalty?" J.Marketing vol. 63, pp.33-44.1999.

Reggiani, A . (ed). 1998, accessibility, trade and locational behavior, Ashgate publishing ltd, England.

Rushe, D. (2013) " The 10 best paid CEO in America". The Guardian , 22 Oct, (online). Available at: http://www.theguardian.com/business/2013/Oct22/best-paid-chief-executives-america (Accessed: 3 May 2014).

Spiekermann and Wegener (2007), update of selected potential accessibility indicators. Final report, urban and regional research (S&W), RRG spatial planning and geoinformation. ESPON. Available online at http:// <www.espon.eu/mmp/online/website/ contentprojects/947/ 1297/file_2724/espon_accessibility_update-2006-fr_070207.pdf>, accessed on 1 July 2009.

Starbucks (2014) Our company available at http:// www. starbucks.com/about- us/company-information (accessed: 3 May 2014).

Shostack, G. Lynn (1984), " Designing Services That Deliver", Harvard Business Review, 62 (January-February), 133-9.

Shostack, G. Lynn (1985), " Planning The Service Encounter ,in the service encounter" , John A. Czepiel, Michael R. Solomon, and Carol F. Suprenant, eds. New York: Lexington Books, 243-54.

Shostack, G. Lynn (1987), " Service Positioning Through, Structural Change", Journal of marketing, 51 (Janurary), 34-43.

Soloman, Michael R. (1985), "Packaging The Service Provider", Service Industries Journal , 5(1), 64-71.

Stevens, C.W. (1980), "K-MartStores Try New Look To Invite More Spending" The Wall Street Journal, Nov. 26, 29-35.

Sullivan, Nicholas P(2007). You can hear me now: How Micro loans and cell phones are connecting the world, San Francisco, CA: John Wilsey & Sans, 2007.

T. Ambler, A. Ioannides, And S. Rose, " Brand s On The Brain : Neuroimages Of Advertising ", Business Strategy rev., vol. 11, 3. pp. 17-30. 2000.

Westbrook, Robert A. (1980), " Intrapersonal affective influences on consumer satisfaction with products, " Journal of consumer research , 7 (

June) 49-54.

Wiig, k.(1993). Knowledge management foundations: Thinking About thinking. How people and organizations create, represent and use knowledge vol.1 , of knowledge management series schema press: Arlington, TX.

World Health Organization (2003). Diet, nutrition and the prevention of Chronic diseases report of a joint WHO/FAO. expert consultation. Geneva: World Health Organization.

Wysocki, B. (1979), " Sight, Smell, Sound: They're all arms in retailer's arsenal" The Wall Street Journal, Nov. 17, 1979. 1-35.

Yale Center For Environmental Law And Policy (2006). Environmental Performance Index. Data available on-line at http://epi.yale.edu

Reference

Adrian, P. (2012). Introduction to marketing theory & practice, 3 rd edition, London: Oxford press.

Ajzen, I (1991). The theory of planned behavior. Organizational behavior and human decision processes, 50(2), 179-211. doi: 10.1016/0749.5978 (91) 90020-7.

Alba, Joseph W. and J. Wesley Hutchinson (1987). " Dimensions Of Consumer Expertise", Journal of consumer research, 13 March, 411-454.

Bailey, L., Mokhtarian, P.L. Little, A. (2008). The broader Connection Between Public Transportation, Energy Conservation And Greenhouse Gas Reduction, Report Prepared As Part Of TCRP Project J-11/Tasks Transit Cooperative Research Program, Transportation Research Board Submitted To American Public Transportation Association in http://www.apta.com/research/into/online/land_use.cfmi, accessed 17 April 2008.

Baucer, R,"Consumer Bhavior As Risk Taking , In Risk Taking And Information handling In Consumer Behavior", D. Coxceds Harvard University Press, Cambridge, Mass 1976.

Biederman, P. (2008). Travel and tourism, Pearson Prentice Hall, New Jersey.

Bogers, R. P., Brug, J. Van Assema, P., & Dagnetie, P.C. (2004) , Explaining fruit and vegetable consumption: The theory of planned behavior and misconception of personal intake level. Appetite, 42,157-166.

Bolton, Ruth N. (1998), " A Dynamic Model Of The Duration Of The Customer's Relationship With A Continuous Service Provider: The Role Of Satisfaction", Marketing Science, 17 (1), 45-65.

B.Shiv and A. Fedorikhin, " Heart And Min In Conflict: The Interplay Of affect And Cognition In Consumer Decision Making", J. Consumer Res., vol. 26, pp. 278-292, Dec. 1999.

Brown, K.W., Ryan, R.M. Reswell , J.D. (2007). Mindfulness: Theoretical Foundatins And Evidence For Its Salutary Effects. Psychological Inquiry, 18, 211-237.

Burke, R.R. : Behavioral effects of digital signage, J. Advertising Res. 49(2), 180-185 (2009).

Cant, M., Brink , A. & Brijall, S., Consumer behavior, Cape Town, South Africa: Juta, 2006.

Conner, M. & Abraham, C. (2001). Conscientiousness and the theory of planned behavior: Toward a more complete model of the antecedents of intention and behavior. Social psychology bulletin, 27, 1547-1561.

Cooper C. Mallon, K, Leadbetter S, Pollack L, Peipins (2005) , cancer internet search activity on a major search engine, United States 2001 to 2003, J Med Internet Res. 7(3): e36.

Cope, R. R. Cope and H. Davis (2008). Disney's virtual Queues: A strategic opportunity to co-brand services ? Journal of Business & economics research, vol. 6 no10, 13-20.

Cornelia, B.F. (1999) Rural development news, the North Central Regional Center For Rural Development vol. no 24 , IOWA.

Couper, M.P. J. Blair and T. Triplet (1999). A Comparison Of Mail And E-mail For a Survey Of Employees In USA Statistical Agencies. Journal Of Official Statistics, 15, 39-56.

David J. Nowak & Gordon M. Melsler (2016) " Air quality effects of urban trees and parks." National recreation and park association, USA.

Data monitor (2008). The proctor and gamble company. Retrieved Nov. 15 2009 from http://www.datamonitor.com/

De Hollander, A. E. M., J.M. Melse, Elebret & P. G.N. Kramers (1999), " An Aggregate public health indicator to represent the impact of multiple environmental exposures" Epidemiology: 606-617.

De Visser, R.O., & McDonnell, E.J. (2013). " Man points": Masculine capital and young men's health. Health psychology, 32(1), 5-14. doi:10. 1037/a0029045.

Dunn, J & A Neumsister (2002). Knowledge management in the Information age. E. business review, Fall , 37-45. Jounral of service, spring 2011, vol. 4, no1, De Grovte (2009).

Dyer, D., F. Dalzell & R. Olegario (2004). Rising tide. Lessons learned from 165 years of brand building at Procter and Gamble. Boston, MA: Havard Business School Press.

Eysenbach G (2006) Infodemiology: Tracking flu- related searches on the web for syndromic surveillance. American Medical Informatics Associaion Annual Symposium Proceedings , Curran Associates, Red Hook, NY, pp. 244-248.

Ettredge M, Gerdes, J. Karuga , G (2005) Using web- based search data to predict macro-economic statistics. Commun ACM 48: 87-92.

Felce, D. and Perry, J. (1995). Quality of life: A contribution to its definition and measurement, vol. 16, no.1 pp: 51-74.

Feldman, Jack M. And John G. Lynch Jr. (1988), "Self-
Generated Validity And Other Effects Of Measurement On Belife, Attitude, Intention And Behavior", Journal of applied psychology, 73(3),421-35.

Fiese, M, Hofmann, W., & Wanke, M (2009). The impulsive consumer. Predicting consumer behavior with implicit reaction time measurement. In M. Wanke (ed.) Social psychology of consumer behavior (pp.335-364). New York, NY: Psychology press.

Fitzsimons, Gavan, J. And Vicki G. Morwitz (1996), " The Effect Of Measuring Intent On Brand-Level
Purchase Behavior", Journal of consumer research, 23 (1), 1-11.

Hallerman , D. (2008) video Advertising Online: Spending And Pricing , New Y ork. E-Marketer.

Harriet Griffey. (2010) The art of concentration, enhance focus, Reduce, stress and achieve move. Macmillan publishers ltd,Basinastoke and Oxford, London UK.

Helleman, D. (2008) Video Advertising Online: Spending And Pricing , New York, E-Marketer.

Hensen, C. (2003). Kreuzfahrtourismus.www.christoph- hensen.de/ Facharbeit.pdf.

Huang, H.I. (2012). An empirical analysis of the strategic Management of competitive advantage: a case study of higher technical and vocational education in Taiwan (Doctoral dissertation,
Victoria University).

Jamieson, Linda F. And Frank M. Bass (1989), " Adjusting Stated Intention Measures To Predict Trial Purchase Of New Products: A Comparison Of Models And Methods," Journal of marketing research, 26 (August), 336-45.

Korea Ministry Of Environment. Public Organizations spend 2.2 Trillon Korean Won To Purchase green Products in 2014; Ministry Of Environment: Sejoung, Korea, 2015.

Kremers, S.P. J., De Bruijn, G.J., droomers, M., Van Lenthe, F. J., & Brug, J. (2005). Environmental interventions for selected dietary behaviors in adults. In J. Brug & F. J. Van Lenthe (eds.) , Environmental determinants and interventions for physical activity, nutrition and smoking: A review pp. 282-315. Rotterdam: Erasmus Medical Center.

Lee, D.; Kim, M. ; Lee, J. adoption of green electricity policies: Investigating the role of environmental attitudes via big data-driven search-queries. Energy policy 2016. 90, 187-201.

Lee, Terrence, " Tech in Asia-connecting Asia's startup system " Tech. in Asia- connecting Asia's startup ecosystem, N.p.,4 July 2016.

Los Angeles Country Department Of public Health (2016), Country Health Ranking Model, Retrieved From
www.countryhealthrankgings.org/our-approach. USA.

Mayne, Lonnie. " Evolve of die in the age of the consumer". Entrepreneur, N.P. , 16 Apr. 2014. web of Oct. 2016.

McGregor, S.L. T., & Goldsmith, E.B. (1998). Expanding our understanding of quality of life, standard of living and well-being. Journal of family and consumer science, 90(2), 2-6, 22.

McMichael, A.J. M. Mckee, J. Shkolnikov and T. Valkanen (2004), " Morality trends and setbacks, global convergence or divergence?", Lancet 363, 1155-1159.

Melse, J.M. & A.E. M. De Hollander (2001). " Human Health And The Environment", background document for the OECD Environmental Outlook, OECD, Paris.

Moschis, George p. & Roy, L. Moore (1979), " Decision making among the young. A socialization perspective " Journal of consumer research , 6 (September).

Mulligan, M. Banerjee, T & Thomas, N. (2008) ,European Paid Content And Activity Forecast, (2008 to 2013), Jupiter Research.

Peter, J., Ryan, M, M, " An Investigation Of Perceived Risk At The Brand Level, " Journal of marketing research, 13 May 1976, pp. 184-188.

Pieters, R., & Wedel, M. (2007). Goal Control Of Visual Attention To Advertising: The Yarbus Implication. Journal Of Consumer Research, 34, 224-233 (August).

Parasuaman, and Leonard L. Berry (1985), " Problems And Strategies In Sevices Marketing", Journal of marketing, 49 (Spring), 33-46.

Priesnitz, W. (2007) Counting Our Food Miles. Natural Life, 1 July.

R.C. Oliver, " When is consumer loyalty?" J.Marketing vol. 63, pp.33-44.1999.

Reggiani, A . (ed). 1998, accessibility, trade and locational behavior, Ashgate publishing ltd, England.

Rushe, D. (2013) " The 10 best paid CEO in America". The Guardian , 22 Oct, (online). Available at: http://www.theguardian.com/business/2013/Oct22/best-paid-chief-executives-america (Accessed: 3 May 2014).

Spiekermann and Wegener (2007), update of selected potential accessibility indicators. Final report, urban and regional research (S&W), RRG spatial planning and geoinformation. ESPON. Available online at http:// <www.espon.eu/mmp/online/website/ contentprojects/947/1297/file_2724/espon_accessibility_update-2006-fr_070207.pdf>, accessed on 1 July 2009.

Starbucks (2014) Our company available at http:// www.starbucks.com/about- us/company-information (accessed: 3 May 2014).

Shostack, G. Lynn (1984), " Designing Services That Deliver", Harvard Business Review, 62 (January-February), 133-9.

Shostack, G. Lynn (1985), " Planning The Service Encounter ,in the service encounter" , John A. Czepiel, Michael R. Solomon, and Carol F. Suprenant, eds. New York: Lexington Books, 243-54.

Shostack, G. Lynn (1987), " Service Positioning Through, Structural Change", Journal of marketing, 51 (Janurary), 34-43.

Soloman, Michael R. (1985), "Packaging The Service Provider", Service Industries Journal , 5(1), 64-71.

Stevens, C.W. (1980), "K-MartStores Try New Look To Invite More Spending" The Wall Street Journal, Nov. 26, 29-35.

Sullivan, Nicholas P(2007). You can hear me now: How Micro loans and cell phones are connecting the world, San Francisco, CA: John Wilsey & Sans, 2007.

T. Ambler, A. Ioannides, And S. Rose, " Brand s On The Brain : Neuroimages Of Advertising ", Business Strategy rev., vol. 11, 3. pp. 17-30. 2000.

Westbrook, Robert A. (1980), " Intrapersonal affective influences on consumer satisfaction with products, " Journal of consumer research , 7 (June) 49-54.

Wiig, k.(1993). Knowledge management foundations: Thinking About thinking. How people and organizations create, represent and use knowledge vol.1 , of knowledge management series schema press: Arlington, TX.

World Health Organization (2003). Diet, nutrition and the prevention of Chronic diseases report of a joint WHO/FAO. expert consultation. Geneva: World Health Organization.

www.ingramcontent.com/pod-product-compliance
Ingram Content Group UK Ltd.
Pitfield, Milton Keynes, MK11 3LW, UK
UKHW041852190726
13854UKWH00002B/850

9 798889 354253